COPYWRITING
MADE SIMPLE

Copywriting Made Simple
How to write powerful and persuasive copy that sells

By Tom Albrighton (abccopywriting.com)
Internal illustrations by Rebecca Osborne (rebeccaosborne.co.uk)
Cover illustration by Ollie Hoff (olliehoff.co.uk)
Page design by Kaarin Wall (kaarin@wizgraphics.co.uk)
Author photograph by Stuart Beard (stuartbeardphotography.co.uk)
Proofread by Liz Jones (ljed.co.uk)

Matador
9 Priory Business Park,
Wistow Road, Kibworth Beauchamp,
Leicestershire LE8 0RX
Tel. 0116 279 2299
Email: books@troubador.co.uk
Web: www.troubador.co.uk/matador
Twitter: @matadorbooks

ISBN 9781789013641
British Library Cataloguing in Publication Data.
A catalogue record for this book is available from the British Library.

Printed and bound by CPI Group (UK) Ltd, Croydon, CR0 4YY

Matador is an imprint of Troubador Publishing Ltd

MIX
Paper from
responsible sources
FSC
www.fsc.org
FSC® C013604

Thank yous

Many thanks to Joanna Tidball, Kevin Mills and Liz Jones for their feedback on the text, and to Leif Kendall, Kate Toon, Dave Trott and Katherine Wildman for kindly endorsing the book.

Thanks to Ollie and Rebecca for their wonderful artwork and to Kaarin for her brilliant design.

Thanks to all my clients, past and present, for supporting my work and helping me develop my skills.

Thanks to everyone I know on Twitter for their enthusiasm, intelligence and humour, and for sharing so many reflections about copywriting and examples of the craft.

Finally, thanks to Mum for the bridge and Dad for the prospectus, and to Karen, Adele and Freddie for their love and support.

COPYWRITING
MADE SIMPLE

How to write powerful and persuasive copy that sells

Tom Albrighton

CONTENTS

PART TWO
WRITE YOUR COPY

What is a headline? · Just say it · Set the theme
Offer a benefit · Create intrigue · Ask a question
Explain why · Break the news · Give a command
Try this: Headline hunt

Why structure matters · Make a plan · Start strong
Write the middle first · AIDA and her daughters
Solve a problem · Give information · Take different views
Family tree · Make a list · Go step by step
The magic of three · Use visuals and formats
Try this: Restructure it

What are calls to action? · Basic calls to action
Bring in benefits and persuasion · Keep it simple
Show that it's quick and easy · Stepping stones
Try this: Call yourself to action

PART THREE
IMPROVE YOUR COPY

What is creativity, and why do you need it?
Creativity with purpose
Some starting points for creative copy · Start simple
Mix it up · See it differently · Find a metaphor
Draw a contrast · Make 'em laugh · Play on words
Use images · Show, don't tell · Stir it up · Do different
Do the opposite · Reframe it · Give it a twist
Switch perspectives · Turn weakness into strength
Get meta · Borrow interest · Be agile
See what others did · Take it further
Try this: Apply your creativity

1

INTRODUCTION

What copywriting is, and how this book can help you do it.

What is copywriting?

There are lots of reasons to write.

You might want to tell a story. Create something beautiful. Express yourself, or share your knowledge. Or you might just enjoy the act of writing itself.

All those reasons are fine. But copywriting is something else.

Copywriting is writing with a job to do. Writing with a practical purpose. Usually, that purpose is to make the reader think, feel or act differently from the way they did before.

Copywriting is like a bridge. On one side is the person who will read your copy. On the other side is you, along with whatever you're selling. Your job is to get the reader to cross the bridge and give it a try.

Now, the reader might not be ready to cross the bridge just yet. They might want to, deep down, but still feel unsure about taking the first step. They might be able to see the other side, or have a vague idea what's over there. Or they might not know the bridge is there at all.

Whatever they're thinking or feeling right now, you've got to change it so they act differently and cross the bridge.

Reader   Copywriter

Cross the bridge

Copywriting is like persuading someone to cross a bridge

Most copy is written to sell products or services, so crossing the bridge means buying or trying something. But you could also be aiming to provide information, explain ideas or build support for a cause. If so, you're trying to get the reader to *buy in* rather than buy – to invest their attention or commitment instead of their cash.

Copy appears in marketing materials like adverts (printed, broadcast and online), sales letters, brochures and websites. It pops up in tweets, posts and updates. It fills articles, white papers and even whole books, as well as other types of content like video scripts and infographics. Wherever words are making things happen for businesses and organisations, that's copywriting.

Sometimes, it can feel like technology has made reading a thing of the past. But while we certainly use many different devices and channels these days, most of what we do on them is still text-based. And marketing messages still have to be written, regardless of how and where people read them. The skill of the copywriter is as important as ever.

The challenge...

Copywriting can be tough. The search for a simple, powerful idea can be long and frustrating. Getting the right ideas in the right order can feel like doing a crossword without the clues. And once you've found words that are powerful and persuasive, you've also got to give them the right personality.

What's more, nobody cares. Your reader isn't eagerly waiting for your copy. In fact, they'd rather not read it at all. You have literally seconds to capture their attention before it jumps to something else.

If your reader is online, they've got plenty more sites to choose from if yours turns out to be dull or confusing.

People are busy, distracted and self-absorbed –
not eagerly awaiting your copy. PHOTO: PIXABAY

If they're on the tube, they'd rather be looking down at their Facebook than looking up at your ad.

If they're at work, they've got a to-do list as long as their arm, and researching your product is just one more thing that's been added to it.

And if they're picking up your mailshot from the doormat, you've got to make your case before they walk from the front door to the recycling bin.

Does that mean copy can never work? Absolutely not. It just means you have to respect your reader, give them something interesting and always remember that they're human.

Legendary copywriter Howard Luck Gossage said, 'People read what interests them, and sometimes it's an ad.'[1] Your job is to hit that sweet spot where your message meets readers' interest – and turn that interest into action.

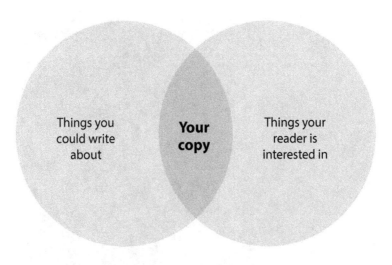

'People read what interests them, and sometimes it's an ad'

---

1   *Changing the World Is the Only Fit Work for a Grown Man* by Steve Harrison, Adworld Press, 2012, p. 52.

...and the reward

So yes, copywriting is challenging. But it's also fun, varied and massively rewarding.

As a copywriter, you create the ideas that give marketing its soul. You decide what brands will say, and how they'll say it. Through your copy, you connect with thousands of people out there in the world, whisper in their ear and offer them something they'll really like. With nothing more than ink on a page, you can change how they think, feel or act. How cool is that?

Then there are the discoveries. All around you, right now, are dreams made solid and real. You'll learn the tiniest details of things you never gave a second thought, and meet people who spend their lives making them. Everywhere you look, there are products waiting to be noticed and have their stories told. You will tell those stories.

The variety can be incredible. You could be writing about diamonds or dog food one day, laptops or luggage the next. You could be thinking up a three-word tagline or dashing off a 300-page ebook. You could be having tea with the local plumber or flying off to interview the CEO of a multinational.

If you do well, you could write for a living. That's something thousands of people dream of. You may not write the next great novel. You may not even write for a brand that anyone's really heard of. But if you love learning, writing and making things happen, you'll love the copywriter's life.

And when your work is done, you'll have the satisfaction of knowing you made a difference. Your client needed your help to capture their ideas, present their product and reach their customers. Your words helped them succeed. You matter.

About this book

As the title of this book suggests, I've aimed to cover the essentials of copywriting as clearly and simply as I can.

You don't have to be a full-time writer, or even write that much, to get something from this book. As far as I'm concerned, if you're writing a classified ad, a job application, a PTA letter or a work presentation, you're copywriting. And you can use exactly the same ideas and techniques as seasoned pros who write for top brands.

Here's how the rest of the book breaks down.

- The first part covers **planning your copy**. It explains how to consider the product, its benefits and your reader, and bring it all together in the brief.
- The second part covers **writing your copy**. It looks at headlines, structuring your copy and calls to action.
- The last part looks at **improving your copy**. It explores how you can make your copy creative, persuasive and engaging; how to maintain a consistent tone; and how to sharpen up your writing and respond to feedback.

You'll notice that there isn't much about the different things you could be writing – adverts, video scripts, sales letters, emails, web pages and so on. That's not because they're all the same, but because there are plenty of techniques you can learn that apply to *all* types of copy. Chapter 17 has some tips on how to apply the ideas to different types of project.

There are examples throughout the book. Some are from real-world brands, and others I've written specially. If the brand name is in italics, or if there's no brand name at all, that means the example is fictitious.

The examples are drawn from companies of every type and every size. I've also tried to feature a fair amount of business-to-business (B2B) copy, as well as business-to-consumer (B2C). B2B copywriting may not be that glamorous, but it's a vital skill (not to mention a huge market) that's often unfairly neglected.

At the end of some chapters are mini tasks, under the heading 'Try this'. They mostly involve thinking rather than writing. Do them if they tickle your fancy.

One last thing. I haven't tried to write the only book you'll read on copywriting – just the first. There are too many sides to copywriting, and too many opinions on it, for one book to cover everything. This is my take, based on my own experience. I've suggested some ideas for further reading in the footnotes throughout the book.

There are online resources to support the book at **copywritingmadesimple.info**, including annotated examples, a reference list (with links) and a bonus chapter.

Enough chat. Your copy won't write itself.

Let's get to work.

PART ONE
PLAN YOUR COPY

2
KNOW THE **PRODUCT**

Understand the product you're writing about.

What are you selling?

Every copywriting project starts with the product you're aiming to sell.

If you're writing for a company, it's going to be one of these four things:

- A **business-to-consumer product** like orange squash or a microwave
- A **business-to-consumer service** like car insurance or window cleaning
- A **business-to-business product** like a photocopier or a forklift truck
- A **business-to-business service** like accountancy or marketing.

Throughout this book, I use the abbreviations 'B2C' for business-to-consumer and 'B2B' for business-to-business.

You could also be 'selling' something that isn't a purchase, like a charity donation. You'll still be able to use many of the techniques in this book, but your copy will be about how the reader can help someone else, as opposed to helping themselves.

Or you might be 'selling' an idea or an opportunity rather than a product. For example, you might be writing an ebook about information security, to encourage business owners to think more seriously about it. Or you might be writing a job ad, to encourage people to apply. Again, you can still use the same approaches, because you want your reader to 'buy in' to what you're saying, or do something other than make a purchase.

Finally, you might be writing copy that simply offers information. It might be a council leaflet about how to claim housing benefit, or a blog post on pruning clematis. In this case, the copy itself is the product, and you 'sell' it by making it as clear and useful as you can.

From now on, to keep things simple, I'm going to call whatever you're writing about 'the product', even though it could be any of the things I've just described.

Understand the product

Whatever the product is, your starting point is to understand it thoroughly. You'll want to think about questions like:

- **What is the product?**
- **What does it do?** How does it work? What problems does it solve? (We'll go deeper into this in the next chapter when we look at benefits.)
- **Who uses it?** How do they use it, and when? How does it fit into their lives – at work, at home or elsewhere?
- **Is there anything unusual, or even unique, about the product?** Is it the only one of its type, or is it the best in some way – fastest, cheapest, most comprehensive? How can that claim be backed up?
- **Why would people buy this product *specifically?*** In other words, what does it offer that rivals don't?
- **How do people buy the product?** Where do they have to go, and what do they have to do? Is buying the product quick and easy or long and complicated?

- **Is there a buying journey?** Is the product an impulse buy (like a fizzy drink) or a planned purchase (like a fridge)? If it's planned, how do people go about researching and deciding?
- **What is the product's position in the market?** Is it basic, regular or premium? Is it newly launched or well established? What are its main competitors?
- **Does the product replace something else?** Is there anything that people would have to stop buying, or stop using, if they chose this product instead? Why might they resist doing that?
- **What might people buy instead?** The alternative isn't necessarily a direct competitor; it could just be something else they might spend money on. For example, cinemas don't really compete with restaurants, but people might still choose between a cinema ticket and a meal out.
- If the product's already on sale, **what do people think of it?** How is it selling? What press coverage and customer reviews has it got? What about the thoughts of people who sell the product – salespeople, retailers, franchisees, brokers and so on?
- If you're writing about a service, **how is it delivered?** Who delivers it? What are their skills, background and personalities, and what does that mean for the customer? Can the customer control or customise the service? Is it completely shaped around their needs?
- Is the product part of a **brand or range?** If so, what rules (written or unwritten) will you need to keep to? How does the brand position itself?
- How do the **history and culture of the company** feed into their product? Is the company an ambitious start-up or an established leader? How is it seen in the market?

These questions could form the basis of a meeting or interview with your client, or even a written questionnaire. You might be surprised that they haven't thought about all these things, at least not consciously. If anything important is still hazy, you need to find it and nail it down – because you can't write about the product otherwise.

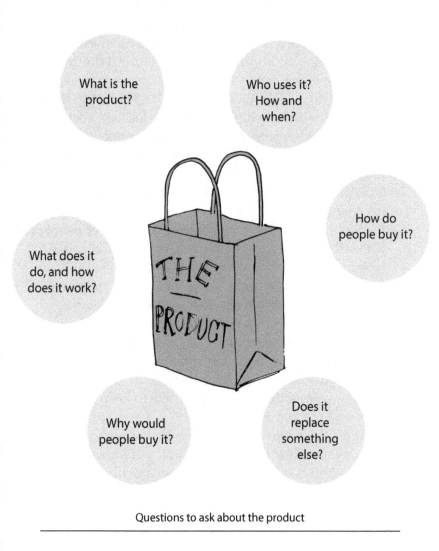

What is the product?

Who uses it? How and when?

How do people buy it?

What does it do, and how does it work?

Why would people buy it?

Does it replace something else?

THE PRODUCT

Questions to ask about the product

Research the product

To learn more about the product, ask the client for all the information they've got – brochures, web pages, internal presentations and anything else. If they offer to write their own notes, say yes. Explain that you don't need their content to be carefully structured or beautifully phrased. Just basic bullet points or random thoughts are fine. You're looking for raw material, not the finished article.

Use the product yourself if you can. Sometimes that's easy: if you're writing about socks, you can wear them, and if you're writing about chocolate, you can taste it. Experiencing a service may be more difficult, particularly if it's expensive or specialised. You may just have to compare it with similar services you have used yourself, or talk to people who have used it. (We'll come back to talking to customers in chapter 4.)

Visit the client

Sometimes, clients will invite you to visit their premises to learn about the product and meet their team. If time, distance and budgets permit, you should definitely go. If nothing else, you'll build a stronger relationship with them, plus you'll almost certainly get some information that you wouldn't otherwise.

Site visits are worthwhile for any product, but are particularly useful for things like professional services. Here, the end client (that is, the client's own client) is really 'buying' the people who'll deliver the service, and the culture of the company will have a big impact on their experience. You'll get a lot closer to that if you visit the firm.

Talk to the client

Client interviews are a great way to generate lots of valuable information in a short time, particularly if your contact isn't keen on writing notes.

In-person interviews are ideal, but phone (or Skype) is a very good substitute. Either way, you might want to record the conversation, so you can concentrate on what's being said without taking notes.

Often, the client will use simple, direct phrases that they'd never put down in writing, but express important truths about the product. Listen out for them, and don't be afraid to put them straight into your copy.

Don't worry about asking really simple, basic questions, like the ones at the top of the list above. You're trying to get information, not look clever. Think of it as role-playing a new customer who knows nothing about the product. You might be surprised at how useful and thought-provoking this is for your client.

Sometimes, you might have most of the information you need, but not enough to write all the copy. If so, you can take a 'fill in the blanks' approach, where you write whatever you can and put in comments indicating where the client needs to help out. This helps to get the project moving forward, and may save the client telling you things that end up not being used.

Too much information?

Most copywriters feel that the more background information they can get their hands on, the better. However, there's another way to look at this.

When you start working on a project, you're encountering the product for the first time, just as your reader will when they read your copy. That perspective can help you see what's truly different or appealing about it, rather than what the client feels is important.

The more product knowledge you have, the easier it is to 'go native' and start seeing things from the client's viewpoint rather than the reader's. You can fall prey to what psychologists call 'the curse of knowledge': the inability to imagine *not* knowing what you know.[2] That can be a real problem if you work for the same client for a long time, and is part of the reason why big brands change creative agencies every so often. You can't be naïve and expert at the same time.

With written material, read what seems useful, but don't get bogged down if it really doesn't seem relevant. Over time, you'll get a feel for what's likely to be valuable. The same goes for interviews. People do ramble, or say stuff that just pops into their heads, even when they're being directly questioned. Don't feel you have to include every last word in your copy.

Some copywriters prefer to throw themselves into the writing, rather than spending ages on research. If that helps you to get your thoughts in order, fine. You don't have to use everything you write, and you can always come back and research in more detail later on.

The strongest argument for working through a lot of background info is that any tiny detail could be the spark that sets fire to your copy. For example, consider this famous headline for Rolls-Royce, written by David Ogilvy:

"At 60 miles an hour the loudest noise in this new Rolls-Royce comes from the electric clock"

Ogilvy spent three weeks reading about the car before he came up with it. If he hadn't put in that time, he never would have found the idea.

2 See tinyurl.com/curseknowledge

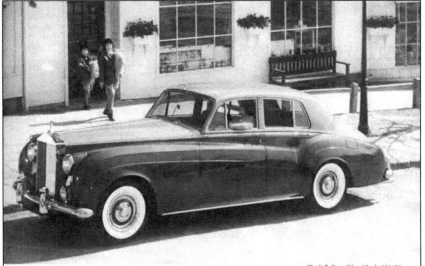

The Rolls-Royce Silver Cloud—$13,995

"At 60 miles an hour the loudest noise in this new Rolls-Royce comes from the electric clock"

What makes Rolls-Royce the best car in the world? "There is really no magic about it — it is merely patient attention to detail," says an eminent Rolls-Royce engineer.

1. "At 60 miles an hour the loudest noise comes from the electric clock," reports the Technical Editor of THE MOTOR. Three mufflers tune out sound frequencies—acoustically.

2. Every Rolls-Royce engine is run for seven hours at full throttle before installation, and each car is test-driven for hundreds of miles over varying road surfaces.

3. The Rolls-Royce is designed as an *owner-driven* car. It is eighteen inches shorter than the largest domestic cars.

4. The car has power steering, power brakes and automatic gear-shift. It is very easy to drive and to park. No chauffeur required.

5. The finished car spends a week in the final test-shop, being fine-tuned. Here it is subjected to 98 separate ordeals. For example, the engineers use a *stethoscope* to listen for axle-whine.

6. The Rolls-Royce is guaranteed for *three*

years. With a new network of dealers and parts-depots from Coast to Coast, service is no problem.

7. The Rolls-Royce radiator has never changed, except that when Sir Henry Royce died in 1933 the monogram RR was changed from red to black.

8. The coachwork is given five coats of primer paint, and hand rubbed between each coat, before *nine* coats of finishing paint go on.

9. By moving a switch on the steering column, you can adjust the shock-absorbers to suit road conditions.

10. A picnic table, veneered in French walnut, slides out from under the dash. Two more swing out behind the front seats.

11. You can get such optional extras as an Espresso coffee-making machine, a dictating machine, a bed, hot and cold water for washing, an electric razor or a telephone.

12. There are three separate systems of power brakes, two hydraulic and one mechanical. Damage to one system will not affect the others. The Rolls-Royce is a very safe car—and also a very lively car. It cruises serenely at eighty-five. Top speed is in excess of 100 m.p.h.

13. The Bentley is made by Rolls-Royce. Except for the radiators, they are identical motor cars, manufactured by the same engineers in the same works. People who feel diffident about driving a Rolls-Royce can buy a Bentley.

PRICE. The Rolls-Royce illustrated in this advertisement—f.o.b. principal ports of entry—costs $13,995.

If you would like the rewarding experience of driving a Rolls-Royce or Bentley, write or telephone to one of the dealers listed on the opposite page.

Rolls-Royce Inc., 10 Rockefeller Plaza, New York 20, N. Y., CIrcle 5-1144.

March 1959

David Ogilvy's Rolls-Royce ad, using a small detail for a big impact.
REPRODUCED BY KIND PERMISSION OF BENTLEY MOTORS LIMITED

TRY THIS

Explore your knowledge

Think of a product you use a lot and really like. It could be a food, a piece of clothing, a gadget or whatever you want.

Now think through all the things you know about it. What do you know about its history, how it's made, where it's sold, who buys it and so on? Is there anything you don't know yet, but would like to?

3

KNOW THE **BENEFITS**

Understand how the features of the product translate into benefits, and which benefits are most important.

Features vs benefits

Imagine we're going on holiday together. You fancy a flashy hotel in Dubai, but I'm yearning for a cosy cottage in the Cotswolds. How could I change your mind?

Maybe I could tell you lots of interesting facts about my cottage:

- The location is just above the Severn Valley.
- It's got a swimming pool.
- There's a pub just down the road.
- It's got two bedrooms.

To me, those things sound great. But I'm already convinced, while you're actively against my idea. To bring you round to my way of thinking, I need to express the same points in a different way:

- You can sip your morning tea and enjoy the view.
- You can keep up with your fitness programme and still have time to relax.
- We can go out for dinner and be home in ten minutes.
- You can sleep in without my snoring disturbing you.

So what's the difference between these two lists?

The first list presents the cottage's *features*, while the second highlights its *benefits*. In other words, while the first list talks about the cottage itself, the second talks about how it helps you.

Why benefits matter

Remember that great quote from Howard Luck Gossage in chapter 1? He said, 'People read what interests them, and sometimes it's an ad.'

There are lots of ways to make your copy interesting, and we'll look at several of them later on. But there's one thing that *everyone* is interested in: themselves. So the simplest way to get their interest is by offering them benefits. Benefits live at the sweet spot where the things you want to say about the product overlap with your reader's self-interest.

Benefits are the heart of effective copywriting. As a copywriter, your most precious resource is your reader's attention. You start out with none, grab whatever you can

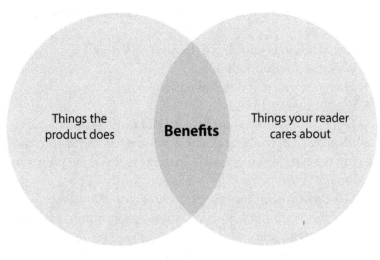

Benefits: the sweet spot where product features meet reader interest

and waste it at your peril. But as long as you're offering your reader a real benefit, clearly expressed, they'll stay with you. On the other hand, if they can't understand the benefit you're offering, or appreciate why it's good for them, they'll walk away.

A big part of planning your copy is deciding which benefits you're going to talk about, and in what order. Some projects, like print ads, might be all about one important benefit. A product description on a website might talk about a few different benefits, but some will still be emphasised more than others.

Turn features into benefits

Benefits are a promise of value. They're the good things that will happen when your reader buys and uses the product.

Marketers have a saying: 'sell the sizzle, not the sausage'.[3] It means that what really sells is the experience of a product, rather than the product itself.

Look back at the benefits of my Cotswold cottage and see how often the words 'you' and 'your' appear. That's because benefits link features to the reader's own experience. They define the relationship between a product and a person, turning the product from a lifeless object into a part of their life.

As a copywriter, one of your most important jobs is to turn features into benefits by making them 'face outwards' towards the reader, so they can clearly see how the product will fit into their life.

Here are some B2C examples of features and the benefits they offer:

---

3   It was coined by US salesman Elmer Wheeler in the 1940s. What he actually said was, 'Don't sell the steak, sell the sizzle.'

	Feature	Benefit(s)
Car parts shop	Big range under one roof	Quick, convenient, only need to make one stop
Winter coat	Fleecy lining	Stay warm and snug in cold weather
Breakfast cereal	Full of oats, high GI	Keeps you going all morning

And a few from B2B:

	Feature	Benefit(s)
New website	Responsive design	Site looks good on any device
Cleaning service	All desks cleaned every night	Tidy workspace, improved hygiene, better impression on visitors
Passcode locks	Individual codes for all staff	Track team members' movements and hours worked

One way to turn features into benefits is to play the role of the reader and ask why different features mean benefits for you. Ask really basic questions like 'How does this product help me?' or 'Why do I need it?' It's easy to lose touch with these fundamentals, but you can't write good copy unless you understand them through and through.

Tangible and intangible benefits

Some benefits are objective and practical, offering the reader things they can see or touch. These are called *tangible* benefits. They can include what the product does, as well as how it does it – speed, convenience, affordability and so on. Tangible benefits are solid, objective facts that readers can use to choose and compare products, or make a logical argument for buying them.

Sometimes you can measure them numerically, like this claim used by Dettol (Reckitt Benckiser):

Kills 99.9% of germs

Other benefits are more subjective and emotional. These are called *intangible* benefits. They offer to change the reader's emotions by making them feel more attractive, secure, clever, fashionable and so on. The famous tagline for L'Oréal promises the intangible benefit of self-esteem:

Because You're Worth It.

Since they only exist in people's heads, you might think intangible benefits are less 'real' than tangible benefits, and therefore less important. But our emotions are very real to us when we feel them, and can be just as powerful as reason – maybe more so.

Tangible benefits	Intangible benefits
Appeal to logic	Appeal to emotion
Happen in people's lives	Happen in people's heads
Solve people's problems	Make people feel better
Can be seen, touched or measured	Can't be seen, touched or measured

Here are a few examples of tangible and intangible benefits.

Product	Tangible benefits	Intangible benefits
Luxury watch	Accurate timekeeping Waterproof Self-winding	Display wealth Impress peers Feel sophisticated
Handwash	Kills 99.9% of germs Handy squeezy bottle Nice lavender scent	Feel that you're keeping family safe and healthy

Product	Tangible benefits	Intangible benefits
Smartphone	Make phone calls Access the internet Use a wide range of apps	Feel connected Feel trendy and up to date
Intelligent thermostat	Save fuel Save money Help the environment	Feel that you're making a difference Impress visitors
Electric drill	Handy mechanism for quick bit changes Rotary and hammer action for a range of materials	Feel skilful and handy round the house Feel the satisfaction of having the proper kit
ISA savings account	Avoid tax on your savings	Feel prepared for the future
Donation to RNLI	Keep the lifeboats going Save lives at sea	Feel that you've helped people Feel that you're giving back to seaside towns you've visited
Office printer management system	Save paper and toner Monitor who prints what	Impress your boss with cost savings Feel informed and in control

Which benefits should you use?

Most products offer some benefits of both types, but the balance you use in your copy will depend on the project.

For example, a website selling office equipment would be almost all about tangible benefits, because that's what B2B buyers want to know about. When people choose insurance, they're mainly interested in value for money, which explains the popularity of comparison sites.

With other products, people decide mainly on intangible benefits, but may still use tangible ones to justify their

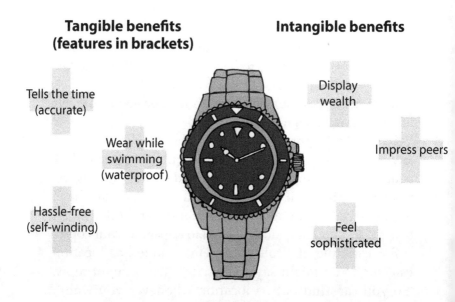

| **Tangible benefits (features in brackets)** | **Intangible benefits** |

Tells the time (accurate)

Wear while swimming (waterproof)

Hassle-free (self-winding)

Display wealth

Impress peers

Feel sophisticated

Tangible and intangible benefits for a luxury watch

choice. Think back to a time when you bought something indulgent, like a gadget or a pair of shoes. You saw it and simply thought: 'I want that.' Then you built up a case in your mind for why you really 'needed' it. You might have used the argument on someone else as well.

Sometimes, a single benefit has both tangible and intangible sides to it. For example, the main tangible benefit offered by the budget supermarket chain Lidl is affordability: savings you can count, cash in your pocket. But because bargain-hunting makes people *feel* thrifty, regardless of how wealthy they are, Lidl attracts plenty of shoppers who could easily afford to go elsewhere.[4]

---

4 'One in three Aldi and Lidl shoppers is "upper or middle class"', *The Telegraph*, 15 March 2015.

So what?

Sometimes, you (or your client) can get caught up in things you want to say about a product, and lose sight of whether they're actually benefits. If you write your copy like that, you'll come across like a pub bore, droning on about yourself while your reader stifles a yawn.

To avoid this, put your benefits to the 'so what?' test. For any feature, keep asking 'so what?' until you get to a clear benefit: a way in which the product definitely makes the reader's life better. If there is no good answer to 'so what?' then you're looking at a feature that doesn't offer much benefit, and probably doesn't need to appear in your copy.

For example, if I told you, 'This phone has location tracking', you might say, 'So what?' Then I might reply, 'So you can find out its location whenever you want', and you might retort, 'So what?' again. Then I could say, 'So you always know where you daughter is, day or night', which is a clear benefit that's 100% about your life rather than the product.

Unique selling points (USPs)

Some products offer benefits that people can't get anywhere else. They might be based on proprietary technology, official endorsements, secret recipes and so on, or they might just be because the product is the first to offer them. Marketers call these unique selling points, or USPs.

You don't necessarily need a USP. But if you do have one, you can make some eye-catching claims in your copy, using words like 'first', 'only', 'cheapest', 'favourite', 'top-selling' or even 'best', if you can justify it. Here's a tweet from Birmingham's Chung Ying Garden restaurant (@ChungYingGarden) that uses the USP of 'widest range':

> Did you know that our kitchen serves the most extensive selection of #dimsum in the UK?

The 'S' in 'USP' is there for a reason: USPs must sell. Having a USP sounds good and is something to be proud of, so companies will sometimes emphasise the unique points of their products even though they don't particularly help their customers. Don't put a feature in your copy just because it's unique. It needs to justify its place with benefits.

The 'U' is there for a reason too: USPs must be unique. It's easy to start throwing the term 'USP' around too casually, or referring to benefits as USPs when they aren't actually unique. Be very clear about what's unique and what isn't, so you don't write something that can't be backed up.

Chung Ying Garden using the USP of 'widest range'

Different benefits can appeal to different users of the same product

Different strokes for different folks

Bear in mind that the same product can offer different benefits to different people, and that the buyer and the user aren't always the same person. While you'll usually be writing your copy to the buyer, other people might benefit from the product too – and they might have a say in the buying decision.

Think about school uniform. For parents, price and durability matter most, but for their kids, comfort and style are more important. A successful product needs to make both groups happy: it's no good buying a sensible cardigan if your child furtively stuffs it into their rucksack the minute they're out of sight.

The same is true in B2B. Say your reader is a team manager considering new accounting software for everyone to use. The team may not be making the buying decision, but they could still influence it. While the manager might be concerned with making working processes more accurate, the team will be more interested in making their own working lives easier. And while the team are thinking only of themselves, the manager might have to convince a superior, like a financial director, who might use the software less than others but will take a keen interest in its total cost of ownership.

Depending on the format you're working in, you might want to address each group of people individually (see 'Take different views' in chapter 7), or point out how the product might benefit people other than the reader.

When features are benefits

If the reader is naturally interested in your features, you may not need to turn them into benefits at all. For 'early adopters' of new technology or keen hobbyists, for example, the feature *is* the benefit.

Let's say you're writing about cameras. For casual users, or people who don't even own a camera yet, you might talk about capturing special moments in vivid colour and pin-sharp detail. But for enthusiasts and professionals, all that stuff goes without saying. They want to know how this camera is measurably better than the one they already have – and that comes down to technical features. If you gloss over them, you're missing out the most important part.

What's more, geekier readers get a kick out of analysing and comparing technical features, and from knowing that they made the best buying decision. So by giving them this type of information, you're offering them an intangible benefit too.

TRY THIS

Turn features into benefits

Choose a product from around your home and think of five of its features. Now re-express them as customer benefits. Use the 'so what?' test to find the most powerful expression of each benefit.

Now, divide your benefits into tangible and intangible. Are they practical or emotional? Do they affect your outer world, or your inner world?

4

KNOW YOUR **READER**

Understand the person you're writing for, inside
and out. Decide what you want them to know,
feel or do when they read your copy.

Who is your reader?

We've looked at the product and identified its benefits. Now it's
time to think about the person who's going to buy it.

When you see TV ads or outdoor posters, it might seem that
they're broadcast at everybody, in the hope that someone will
be interested. In fact, most marketing only speaks to a few of
the people who actually see it. And that's completely deliberate.

You can't be all things to all people. If you try to appeal
to everybody, you'll end up appealing to nobody. Instead,
you should focus on the people who are most likely to
appreciate the product and its benefits, because they'll be the
easiest to persuade.

To keep things simple, I'm going to call the target of your copy
your *reader*, even though they might hear your words in a TV or
radio ad, or see your idea in a design that has no words at all.

As Stephen R. Covey says, if you want to communicate
effectively, you should 'seek first to understand, then to be

understood'.[5] If you don't really know who your reader is, you won't be able to write for them. Or you might end up writing copy to please yourself, or your client. That might get your copy approved, but it won't bring in any extra sales.

Let's look at three ways to think about your reader: how they live, what they want and how they feel.

How does your reader live?

You can identify your reader by their personal profile. Here are a few characteristics you could use.

Identify readers by their...	For example...
Age, gender	People born after 1990 Women over 30
Family situation	Parents of children under 10 Grown-up children still living at home
Social situation	People with a wide circle of friends they see regularly
Work	Middle managers in the public sector
Location	People who live in rural Wales
Finances	Homeowners with household income over £50,000pa
Habits	People who always leave the heating on
Problems	People whose eyesight is failing People who can't fix their own computers
Interests	People who like role-playing games People who play tennis
Cultural tastes	People who listen to grime and bashment
Opinions	People who think Jeremy Clarkson talks a lot of sense

---

5   This is the fifth habit in Covey's book *The 7 Habits of Highly Effective People: Powerful Lessons in Personal Change*, Simon & Schuster, 2004.

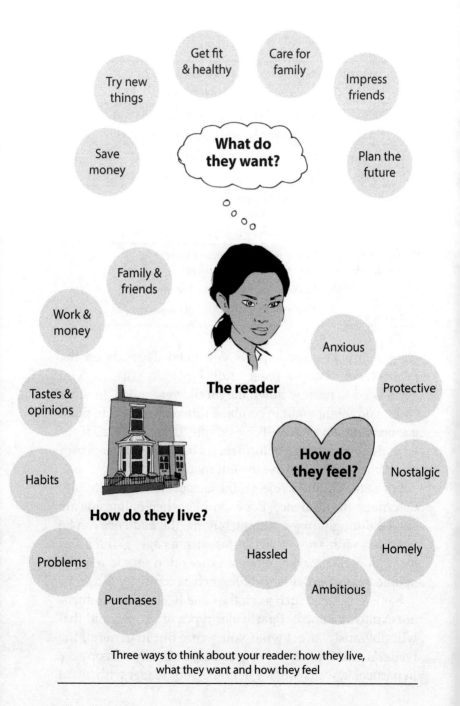

Three ways to think about your reader: how they live,
what they want and how they feel

Identify readers by their...	For example...
Buying choices	People who shop at Waitrose
	People who wear Stone Island
Buying preferences	People who go on active holidays
	People who keep up with new technology
Buying habits	People who never shop online
	People who only ever buy new cars
Product knowledge	People who don't know about the Internet of Things
	People who've bought from the brand before
Online behaviour (using data from website analytics, social media and so on)	People who put things in their basket but don't buy them
	People who tweet about *The Voice*
	People who stream a lot of Rihanna

How many of these aspects you need depends on the product. For example, most adults buy toilet paper, so you don't need to narrow down the profile very much. In other cases, you might want to combine different aspects to paint a more detailed picture. For example, the target reader for an online accounting platform might be 'owner-managers of small businesses who use the internet a lot'.

For some digital projects, these aspects might literally determine the audience. For example, when online ads are served through programmatic buying, the audience can be specified with known attributes such as age, gender and location, while marketing emails are often sent to a list of people with a particular profile, such as company directors.

Some products, such as clothes and healthcare products, are explicitly aimed at particular types of people, and that will obviously affect what you write. But in general, the reader's profile probably isn't enough to base your copy on. In particular, watch out for defining your reader with broad terms like 'millennials' or 'retirees', and nothing else. You'll end up writing for a stereotype, or assuming that readers will respond just because of who they are. It's much more effective to look at what the reader *wants* and *feels*.

What does your reader want?

You've got a sense of how your reader looks from the outside. But what about their inner life? What's going on for them right now? What do they want to bring into their lives, and what would they rather be rid of?

Here are a few possibilities, for both everyday consumers (B2C) and business buyers (B2B).

B2C version I want to...	B2B version We want to...
Get a job done more easily	Improve task effectiveness
Have more free time	Improve efficiency
Make money	Grow the business
Save money	Reduce overheads
Try something new and different	Develop innovative products or services
Have fun, indulge myself	Improve the working environment
Get away from it all	Reduce stress, boost motivation
Sort my life out	Troubleshoot internal systems and processes
Make my home nicer	Improve infrastructure or premises
Look after my family	Improve employees' wellbeing
Get fit	Build new skills
Plan for my future	Develop business strategy
Feel attractive	Build the brand
Feel trendy	Enhance the firm's reputation

B2C version I want to…	B2B version We want to…
Impress friends	Build personal reputation
Get ahead	Get a competitive edge

I've put these two side by side to show that B2B readers aren't so different from B2C ones. Yes, they're thinking about different things, because they're at work. But they're thinking about them in much the same way, because they're still the same people, with the same kinds of needs and desires.

Notice that these things might cut across the real-life characteristics in the previous section, which makes them more flexible and powerful. Depending on the product, you might not even need any personal details at all to identify your reader. For example, *anyone* might want to get fit or impress their friends – no matter who they are, how they live or what else is going on in their life.

Another useful angle on what the reader wants is their 'jobs to be done'. The idea came out of research by American academic Clayton M. Christensen and others into the best way for firms to create new products and services.[6] Jobs to be done are the things that people want to accomplish, or the experiences they want to create. They 'hire' products to do their jobs, keep them on if they perform well and fire them if they don't. Jobs to be done can be small (like making ice cubes) or large (like finding a new home).

Thinking about jobs to be done keeps your focus firmly on the reader and what they want. Christensen gives the example of a construction firm designing luxury homes for retirees to downsize into. Sales were slow, and analysing customers' profiles or the benefits of the homes failed to

---

6   'Know Your Customers' "Jobs to Be Done"' by Clayton M. Christensen, Taddy Hall, Karen Dillon and David S. Duncan, *Harvard Business Review*, September 2016 (tinyurl.com/customersjobs).

show why. In the end, the company realised that buyers wanted space for their dining-room tables, so their families could still gather in their homes at Christmas. The firm wasn't building homes; it was moving lives.

Jobs can also reveal the true competitors to a product. Say the reader wants to fill an idle 45 minutes on a train. A smartphone game could do that job. But so could a magazine, a podcast or an album. The reader could even get the job done after a fashion by just staring out of the window, and not buying anything at all. The game's rivals aren't only other games in the App Store, but other 'applicants' for the job to be done; other ways for the reader to create the experience they want. Thinking through these points can help you decide which benefits to highlight in your copy, or the right way to describe them.

As these examples show, what the reader wants doesn't necessarily match up neatly with the product, or what it does. As Basecamp founder Jason Fried says, 'Before someone goes buying, there's a reason they go shopping.' He calls this first motivation 'the why before the why'.[7] Before people have a reason to buy products (the second 'why'), there's a situation they want to change (the first 'why'). As a copywriter, your job is to uncover the first 'why' and link it to the second in a convincing way.

If you're writing copy to provide information or help deliver a service, you may find user stories and job stories useful.[8] User stories take the form 'As a [role], I want to [action] so I can [goal].' Here's an example for a healthcare information website:

> As a concerned parent, I want to research symptoms quickly so I can decide whether to call the doctor.

7   See tinyurl.com/friedwhy
8   Both user stories and job stories are explained in detail in *Content Design* by Sarah Richards, Content Design London, 2017, pp. 91–108.

Job stories are similar, but focus more on the reader's 'job to be done'. They take the form 'When [situation], I want to [action] so I can [goal].' As we've seen, this approach can be more flexible, because it accepts that people's needs are changeable and may not depend on who they are. For example:

> <u>When</u> a child is ill, <u>I want to</u> research symptoms quickly <u>so I can</u> decide whether to call the doctor.

Now the story works for *anyone* who might be worried about an ill child – a teacher, a childminder, a grandparent and so on.

Stories like this give you a good test of whether your copy is fit for purpose. In the examples above, the website needs to describe symptoms, say what they mean and explain what to do next. Also, the copy needs to be short (because readers are in a hurry) and very clear (because they may be agitated or upset, making it hard to concentrate).

How does your reader feel?

At the deepest level is how your reader feels about themselves and their life. And the key to understanding that is empathy.

Empathy means getting right inside someone else's experience. It's not just an intellectual analysis of how they think or act. When you truly empathise with someone, you see what they see and feel what they feel. You take an imaginative leap of faith, surrender control and accept that you might be changed by what you experience.

Recently, researchers have found that we feel empathy in the same part of our brain as physical pain.[9] So when you empathise with someone, you're literally 'feeling their pain'.

---

9 'Differential pattern of functional brain plasticity after compassion and empathy training' by O.M. Klimecki, S. Leiberg, M. Ricard and T. Singer, *Social Cognitive and Affective Neuroscience*, vol. 9(6), 2014, pp. 873–879.

Empathy is emotional listening. When you respect someone else's feelings, they know that you're hearing them, that you acknowledge their experience and their personal reality. Then they're much more likely to listen to what *you've* got to say.

Obviously, you can't actually 'listen' to your reader as an individual person. You're creating a one-way communication that has to reach many different people at once. But you can still do your best to see the world – or at least the product – the same way they do.

Here are some questions to think about.

- How does your reader see themselves – now, and in the future?
- How do others see them? How do they *think* others see them? And how would they like to be seen?
- Who would they like to be?
- What makes them feel good or bad? What do they want more of, and less of, in their life?
- What are they looking forward to? What do they look back on fondly?
- What problems are they trying to solve? What's stopping them from reaching their goals, and how?
- What threats are they facing? What could make their life worse, and what power do they have to resist or change it?
- What's on their mind right now? Is there anything they're trying *not* to think about? What keeps them awake at night?
- How do they see the world? What makes them feel happy, sad, angry, compassionate, excited, safe, anxious, nostalgic, regretful, hassled, frustrated, apprehensive, fired up, adventurous?
- What do they feel about the product or brand you're writing about – or similar ones?

Empathy isn't just fairy dust that you sprinkle on top of something you were going to say anyway. It should be at the very heart of your message.

Anaïs Nin said, 'We do not see things as they are, we see them as we are.'[10] You can present all the objective facts and rational arguments you want, but if what you say goes against your reader's beliefs, they're unlikely to listen. Psychologists call this confirmation bias: people latch on to information when it confirms what they already know or believe, and reject it if it challenges their worldview. People don't walk around looking to have their minds changed.

That's why your job is not to drag the reader across the bridge against their will, but to see things from their side and make them *want* to cross. We'll come back to this idea in chapter 13, when we look at persuasion.

However, not every purchase is driven by deep emotions. Sometimes, people just want a product to do a job, and their involvement doesn't go much deeper than that. For example,

Ronseal®'s famous slogan empathised with homeowners who just wanted to get the job done. REPRODUCED BY KIND PERMISSION OF RONSEAL® UK

---

10 To be more precise, a character in her book *The Seduction of the Minotaur* (Sky Blue Press, 2010) reflects on this phrase, although Nin attributes it to the Jewish Talmud.

people buy Ronseal® because they need to preserve their woodwork. They want a product that's affordable, easy to apply, lasts a long time and looks good – and that's it. The brand's famous slogan perfectly positions the product as the answer to that need:

Does exactly what it says on the tin.

Does that mean Ronseal® buyers don't feel any emotion? Absolutely not. It's simply that their feelings come from the brand's solid, practical appeal. When homeowners choose Ronseal®, they feel the relief and gratitude of finding a product that 'just works'.

Research the reader

The most direct way to get to know the reader is to talk to people who already use the product, or one like it. They may tell you why they like the product, or how it helps them, which helps you empathise with them. (They may even talk about some drawbacks, suggesting objections you need to address, or areas to steer clear of.) If you can't reach customers through the client, someone among your family, friends or work colleagues may have used the product, or something like it.

However, bear in mind that people may never express the emotions that make them buy a product – not to you, not to their friends, not even in their own heads. They'll give a rational answer if you ask them, but it may not be what actually motivates them. So it's important to consider what customers do, as well as what they say.[11]

A similar point applies to B2B. Many companies say they are all about quality or innovation, but when you come to work with them, you may discover that they're actually far

11 For research showing why this is so, see 'The margarine test: why marketers must look at what people do rather than what they say' by Richard Shotton, *The Drum*, 14 November 2017.

more concerned with reducing cost and avoiding risk. You can empathise much better with a B2B reader when you understand the company culture they probably work in.

There are other angles you can take to get a more rounded perspective. The client might have some market or industry research that you can read. You might be able to talk to those who deal with customers and know them best, like salespeople, admin teams or customer service staff. The things you find out may not be true of all buyers everywhere, but they'll still be a useful starting point.

Online resources can help too. Browsing forums like Mumsnet, or reviews at shopping sites like Amazon, can show you what people are saying about different types of product, both positive and negative. For something more specific to your project, you could post a question for real people to answer at Quora (quora.com), Yahoo Answers (answers.yahoo.com) or Answers.com.

Write a persona

If you like, you can develop your reader profile into a more detailed description of a (fictitious) individual. Marketers call this a persona. Here's an example persona for trendy headphones:

Ella, an imaginary user of trendy headphones. Using images can make marketing personas feel more real and human. PHOTO: PIXABAY

Ella is 16, lives at home and has enough disposable income to buy some electronic gear. She loves music and listens whenever she can, at home and when out and about.

For Ella, music is more than an interest or an accessory; it's a way of expressing her identity. She wants to feel part of her social circle, but at the same time she wants to stand out through little individual touches.[12] She likes good-quality stuff, but not if it's ostentatious or flashy. Above all, she doesn't want anything her parents would buy.

Another approach is to think about the reader's typical day. What do they do, where do they go and who do they see? What do they read, watch or listen to? What do they think and feel? What marketing messages do they hear, and what do they think about them?[13]

Personas have both pros and cons. They can help you write for your reader as an individual, which is good (as we'll see in chapter 11). But a detailed persona might also lead you to believe that its characteristics are more common than they really are (what psychologists call the 'conjunction fallacy'[14]). However convincing your imaginary reader may be, they still don't actually exist. And while there may be many other customer profiles that are equally important and valid, a persona narrows your view to just one.

12 For research showing how young adults like to fit in and stand out at the same time, see 'How national culture impacts teenage shopping behavior: Comparing French and American consumers' by Elodie Gentina, Raphaëlle Butori, Gregory M. Rose and Aysen Bakir, *Journal of Business Research*, 2013.
13 For a set of detailed and very funny personas from Middle England, see *The Middle Class Handbook*, Not Actual Size, 2010.
14 See *Thinking, Fast and Slow* by Daniel Kahneman, Penguin, 2012, p. 158ff.

Set your aim

Having worked out where you reader is now, you need to decide where you want them to be. How do you want your copy to affect them? What you want them to *know*, *feel* or *do* as a result of reading it?

Most copywriting is about selling a product, in which case you obviously want your reader to buy it. That's the doing part. But it's not always that simple. There might be some knowing or feeling that has to happen too, on the way to a sale.

First, you might have different bits of copy for different stages of the customer journey (or 'sales funnel'), and each bit might have a different aim. For example, if you were selling double glazing, you might write an online buyer's guide explaining the different kinds of window, which would give readers information (knowing) and build their trust in the brand (feeling), but not directly promote the product. Then you could link to a landing page encouraging people to get in touch for a quote (doing). Pushing website visitors to get a quote straight away might turn off those who aren't quite ready to commit, or those who need more information about what they're buying.

Second, you might not be selling a product at all. You might be writing for a charity, in which case your aim might be to tell readers about your cause (knowing), then get them to sympathise with it (feeling) and make a donation (doing). Coming straight out and asking them to give probably wouldn't work so well.

Third, your aim might be to build awareness of a brand, not sell a product as such. For this type of project, you want people to remember the brand (knowing) in a positive light (feeling), so that when the time does come to buy, they're more likely to choose it. But you're not directly asking them to do anything right now.

Finally, you might be writing for a public-sector organisation that wants to tell people about its services. So you just want readers to know the information, and not feel or do anything in particular.

Here are a few examples:

| | What you want the reader to... | | |
	Know	Feel	Do
TV ad for cheesy snacks	The snacks are really tasty and made with real cheese	'Those look nice – I'd like to try them'	Buy the snacks
Double-glazing buyer's guide	Different types of window and how they suit different properties	'This guide seems useful and trustworthy' 'Maybe we should get new windows'	Click through to landing page
Double-glazing landing page	How we can provide and fit any type of double glazing	'We really need new windows' 'I wonder what it would cost?'	Complete online enquiry form
Mailshot for a wildlife charity	The plight of native birds in winter	'Poor birds! I'd like to help them'	Make a donation
No-copy perfume ad	—	'I want to be like her'	Buy the perfume
Government website about tax	How new tax laws affect you	—	Read the website itself

Whatever your aim, you also need to bear in mind where and how the reader will see your copy. Will it interrupt them while they're doing something else, or will they seek it out? There's a big difference between actively searching for a product online and seeing a poster on the street.

TRY THIS

Readers and aims

Check out a few adverts on TV, online or when you're out and about.
Who are they targeted at? How can you tell?
Do they take account of what the reader is doing as they read?
What desires or feelings do they appeal to?
What are they trying to get the reader to think, feel or do?

5

WRITE THE **BRIEF**

Sum up the product, its benefits,
your reader and your aims in the brief.

What is the brief?

We've looked at the product, its benefits, the reader and
what we want them to do. Now we can bring those things
together into a written brief for our copywriting project, as
shown in the diagram (overleaf).

A copywriting brief is simply a document that says what
your copy needs to do. It's the mission statement for your
copywriting project, helping you know your destination
before you set off.

The brief is the yardstick for evaluating your copy. As you
write, you can look at your copy and ask yourself, 'Does this
answer the brief, or part of the brief?' If it does, great. If it
doesn't, either your copy needs to change, or the brief may
not be right.

Agreeing the brief helps you keep your work on track.
Copywriting projects can run into problems if the different
people involved don't agree on what the copy should be
doing. If you sort that out upfront, things usually go more
smoothly later on.

*Turn features
into benefits*

Benefits
How does the product
help people?

The product
What is it?
What does it do?

*Make benefits relevant and
interesting to the reader*

Aim
What do you want
the reader to know,
feel or do?

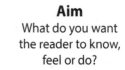

The reader
How do they live?
What do they want?
How do they feel?

Influence the reader

The basic elements of a copywriting brief

Who writes the brief?

If you're working direct for the client, they may write you a brief, or they may just have a few ideas jotted down. They may provide nothing at all, expecting you to take the lead. Whatever happens, it's up to you to obtain a usable brief, even if that means writing it yourself and getting the client to approve it.

If you're working through an agency, they may put together a brief on the client's behalf. If not, you should be able to chat the project through with them and get a clear idea of what's required. Or they may ask you to speak to the client directly. Again, it's all good, as long as you get the information you need.

As time goes by, you'll probably be able to hold the brief in your mind without putting it down on paper, particularly on smaller projects. Or you might feel that writing a brief, or even discussing it, just holds up the project when you could be getting on with the writing. But there's no harm in writing down the brief, even if you're working completely alone. It's a very good way to focus your thoughts and mobilise your mental resources.

What goes into a brief?

Here are some things that could go into a copywriting brief, beginning with the essentials and moving on:

Product:
- What is the product?
- Who is it for?
- What does it do?
- How does it work?
- How do people buy and use it?

Benefits:
- How does the product help people?
- What are its most important benefits?

Reader:
- Who are you writing for?
- How do they live?
- What do they want?
- What do they feel?
- What do they know about the product, or this type of product?
- Are they using a similar product already?

Aim:
- What do you want the reader to do, think or feel as a result of reading this copy?
- What situation will they be in when they read it?

Format:
- Where will the copy be used? (Sales letter, web page, YouTube video, etc)
- How long does it need to be? (500 words, 10 pages, 30 seconds, etc)
- How should it be structured? (Main title, subtitles, sidebars, pullout quotes, calls to action, etc)
- What other types of content might be involved? (Images, diagrams, video, music, etc)

Tone:
- Should the copy be serious, light-hearted, emotional, energetic, laid-back, etc?

Constraints:
- Maximum or minimum length
- Anything that must be included or left out
- Legal issues (regulations on scientific or health claims, prohibited words, trademarks, etc)
- How this copy needs to fit in with other copy that's already been written, or that will be written in the future
- Whether the copy will form part of a campaign, so that different ideas along the same lines will be needed in future (see 'Take it further' in chapter 9)
- Which countries the copy will appear in (whether in

English, or translated)
- SEO issues (for example, popular search terms that should feature in headings)
- Brand or tone of voice guidelines (see 'Tone of voice guidelines' in chapter 15)

Other background information about:
- The product (development history, use cases, technical specifications, distribution, retail, buying processes, buying channels, marketing strategy)
- The product's market position (price point, offers and discounts, customer perceptions, competitors)
- The target market (size, history, typical customer profile, marketing personas)
- The client (history, current setup, culture, people, values)
- The brand (history, positioning, values)

Project management points:
- Timescales (dates for copy plan, drafts, feedback, final copy, approval)
- Who will provide feedback, and how
- Who will approve the final copy, and how
- How the copy will be delivered (usually a Word document, but not always)

These are only suggestions. There's no preset format, structure or length for a brief. It could be a long, formal document that goes into exhaustive detail on all the points above. Or it could be a short exchange of emails. What matters is that you get the information you need, and agree the aims of the project with the client.

An example brief

Here's an example of a basic copywriting brief, focusing on the copy to be written rather than how the project will be managed:

Copy brief:
Landing page for *Wind-O* double glazing

Write a 750–1000-word landing page to promote *Wind-O*'s sealed-unit double glazing (SUDG) manufacture and installation service.

We want to target middle-aged and retired owners of older homes who have some disposable income or savings. They've thought about fitting double glazing to improve the appearance, soundproofing and/or energy economy of their homes. They also have an eye on property value, though more for leaving a legacy than moving home.

They're wary of flashy salesmen and cowboy companies. They want to feel they've made a wise choice. They value service and want to be treated with care and courtesy. They probably won't have bought double glazing before, so they won't know the process.

Explain why SUDG is a good idea in principle, and why *Wind-O* products are technically superior. Mention our strong market position (ranked fifth by sales), the affordability of our products and the breadth of our range. Describe our service step by step, and explain how it makes the whole process as easy and hassle-free as possible. Use a selection of edited customer testimonials and mention our 30-day money-back guarantee.

Encourage people to fill in the online form to request a quote. Include calls to action throughout the page. Use subheadings and pullouts to reach skim-readers.

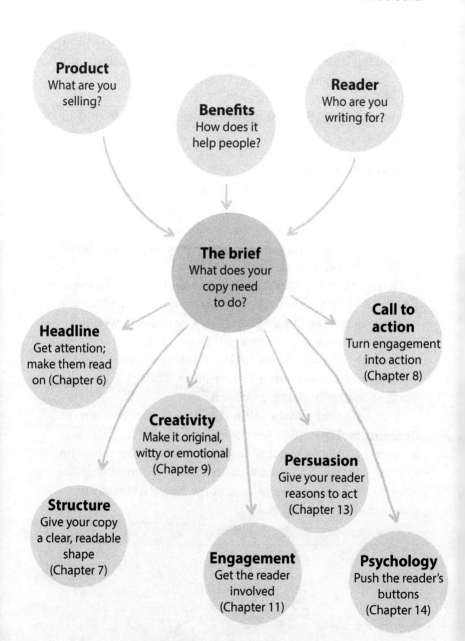

How your aim comes together in the brief,
before you explore the different ways to answer it

We'll be looking at some of the things mentioned here in more detail later on. The 'step by step' structure is discussed in chapter 7, while calls to action are in chapter 8. Persuasive techniques, including authority (the market positioning) and social proof (the customer testimonials) are covered in chapter 13.

One job, one brief

Each copywriting job needs one simple, clear brief. It's easy to place too many demands on a piece of copy, or set aims that are actually in conflict with each other. Thinking and talking about the brief is a great way to iron out those problems before you start.

That's not to say there's only one way to write the copy. There could be hundreds, and every copywriter will have a different way of tackling a project. And you might well want to explore several approaches to the same brief, particularly for projects like adverts or taglines. But that's the *how*, not the *what* – execution rather than strategy. The brief stays the same no matter how you answer it.

As the diagram shows, setting the brief is about *convergent* thinking: making either/or decisions to home in on a clear and simple plan. Once the brief is decided, you move on to *divergent* thinking: exploring the many different ways to answer the brief and write your copy. And that brings us to the second part of the book.

PART TWO
WRITE YOUR COPY

6

WRITE YOUR **HEADLINE**

Grab readers' attention and make them want to read on.

What is a headline?

Your headline is the short phrase or sentence that starts your copy. It could be the slogan of a magazine advert or poster, the subject line of an email, the title of a blog post, the main heading of a web page and so on.

Marketing headlines have the same job as headlines in newspapers and magazines: to grab attention and make people want to read on. David Ogilvy found that five times as many people read the headline as read the body copy.[15] So it's worth spending time on yours, because it might be your only chance to get your message across. In fact for some projects, like outdoor posters, the headline might be all the copy there is.

Writing good headlines can be hard, even for experienced copywriters. Sometimes, it's easier to write the body copy first, then go back and think about the right headline for it. It can also be worthwhile generating a few different ideas, then comparing them and choosing the best one.

15 *Ogilvy on Advertising* by David Ogilvy, Prion, 2014, p. 71.

This chapter looks at some tried and tested types of headline that work in lots of situations. In chapter 9, we'll see how you can be a bit more adventurous.

Just say it

The simplest type of headline simply says what the product is, and what it does. The basic formula is '[Product] is a [description] that helps you [action].' For example:

> Amazon Dash Button is a Wi-Fi-connected device that reorders your favourite product with the press of a button.

The great thing about this approach is that it's completely transparent. It makes a very clear offer to readers, who can then decide whether they want to read on. As well as being effective, that also gives a positive impression of honesty and simplicity.

Simple descriptive headlines are also a good choice for information projects, where you want to tell the reader exactly what your copy is about. For example:

> How to fix a burst water pipe with basic household tools

Whatever the aim of your project, straight descriptions work well for SEO, when you want Google's algorithms to list your page for a particular subject, and make sure people click through to it from search results.

Set the theme

Headlines are conversation starters: they tell readers what you want to talk about. In most cases, you'll want your reader to know what your copy is about straight away, so they understand that it's aimed at them. If they don't, they may stop reading, and your message may never reach them.

Be specific. Remember, you don't want attention from everybody – only the readers you identified in chapter 4.

Trying to get attention from everybody will just dilute the impact of your headline, so you end up getting attention from nobody.

Headlines also set the tone for the rest of the copy. If your headline is jokey, or dark, or businesslike, that suggests that whatever follows will carry on in the same style. So you're not only telling the reader what you're going to say, but how you're going to say it too.

The headline/subheadline opening from Basecamp's home page is a great example of a specific, theme-setting headline:

> **Basecamp solves the critical problems that every growing business deals with.**
>
> It's the saner, calmer, organized way to manage projects and communicate company-wide.

Straight away, we know this page is aimed specifically at owners or managers of young firms, who need help with projects and communication. Those readers sit up and listen; everyone else tunes out and leaves the page. And that's exactly what Basecamp wants.

100,000+ paying customers   Sign in Learn Support Pri

Basecamp
2017 is the year to get it together

Basecamp solves the critical problems that every growing business deals with.

It's the saner, calmer, organized way to manage projects and communicate company-wide.

Basecamp's home-page headline makes the theme crystal clear.

Offer a benefit

When readers come to a piece of copy for the first time, they're thinking, 'What's in this for me?' At that stage, they're not even asking what they could get from the product, but whether it's even worthwhile reading the rest of your copy. So your headline is the 'ad for the ad', in the same way as a cover is the ad for a book.

The best way to draw the reader in is by including a benefit in your headline. A benefit headline says, 'Hey, here's something you might like. Can I tell you about it?' Nothing interests like self-interest, which is why headlines with benefits work so well.

Here are a few examples of headlines that offer benefits while also targeting specific readers and introducing the product.

Brand	Headline	Target reader	Benefits offered
Spoke London	Properly made clothes that really fit, direct from the workshop	Style-conscious men, probably aged 20–50, who don't mind buying clothes online	Quality Comfort Affordability (implied by 'direct from the workshop')
Riverford	Organic veg boxes from our farm to your table	Health-conscious cooks who care about the environment	Cook tastier, healthier food Easy buying process
MyFitnessPal (Under Armour)	Lose Weight with MyFitnessPal The fastest, easiest to use calorie counter app.	Anyone who uses apps and wants to lose weight	Get slim and healthy Ease of use

Brand	Headline	Target reader	Benefits offered
RSPB	Homes for Nature Fund You can give nature the space it needs to survive and thrive	People concerned about nature and the environment	Help a good cause Feel virtuous
Bytestart	60-second guide to Value Added Tax (VAT) for start-ups and small businesses	Company owners who need to know about VAT	Get valuable knowledge Save time

Don't try to cram too many benefits into your headline. Feature one, or two at the most, and unpack the rest in the body copy. If you feel there are lots of equally important benefits you need to state upfront, you can use a headline/subheadline approach, like MyFitnessPal.

With content marketing articles like the Bytestart example above, the benefit lies in the knowledge, interest or entertainment value of the copy itself. In Bytestart's case, the headline promises to get useful info across super quick, which is a benefit in itself and shows empathy with the frantic life of the start-up founder.

Create intrigue

Keeping readers reading is a big part of copywriting. In fact, you could even say that your *only* job is to make people read the next sentence. Keep that up right to the end of your copy and you're doing pretty well.

As we've seen, offering a benefit is a tried and trusted way to draw the reader in. But it's not the only way to go. You could also write something less direct that piques readers' curiosity. Then, as they 'lean in' and start reading, you reveal more details, linking the headline to the product and throwing in some benefits. For example:

10% Battery Remaining.

Those were the last words I wanted to see that Tuesday morning. I was on the way to a major pitch and we were finalising our proposal over email. If my phone died, our hopes of closing the deal died with it.

If only I'd known about the *PhoneZing* portable battery pack – or, better still, had one in my briefcase. I would have had enough juice for ten trips to London, and as many emails as I could type.

With this sort of approach, you're gambling short-term relevance in the hope of winning longer-term interest. A headline like '10% Battery Remaining' doesn't say much about the product, but it does speak directly to an experience that relevant readers have probably had. If the gamble pays off, they'll be more absorbed and curious upfront than they might have been with a simple benefit headline (like 'Charge your phone on the go').

Ask a question

Do questions work in headlines? Yes, as long as readers answer the way you want them to.

The simplest approach is to ask a leading question that invites a yes/no response.

Want to save money on your home insurance?

The answer's pretty obvious, and actually this is just a slightly more involving way to say 'Save money on your home insurance'. But that unspoken 'yes' from the reader still makes the difference between passive acceptance and active agreement.

The next level up is something with a bit more emotional power, like these questions from Cleanhome:

Fed up with housework?

Do you work long hours?

Are you too tired to clean?

Would you rather spend time with
your friends and family?

These get closer to the things we explored in chapter 4: the reader's personal situation, how they feel about it and what they'd like to change. Notice how the questions lead the reader along a logical path from where they are (working), then to the result of that (too tired) and finally to a high-level benefit of the product (more quality time).

However, make sure you don't overdo it. Questions can be confrontational, plus they force the reader to think. So if you ask too many in a row, the reader may start to feel a bit hassled. Instead of interrogating a reader who can't actually answer, move on to what you've got to say to them.

Other questions encourage readers to reflect more deeply on themselves and their situation. In neuro-linguistic programming (NLP) they're called 'meta model questions'. They usually begin with 'what' or 'how', inviting a thoughtful, descriptive answer rather than 'yes' or 'no'.

For example, the UK Post Office®'s tagline asked people to imagine how they could use the postal service:

What will <u>you</u> send?

This Farmfoods headline does a similar thing, but links the question to a benefit (low price):

What will <u>you</u> do with the money you save?

By asking a question like this, you can prompt the reader to start speculating about their future. Then your copy positions the product as the first step towards making that future a reality.

Not all questions work as well as this. One that can cause problems is 'why not?':

Why not try our new fixed-price lunch menu?

The benefits of the menu are clear: affordability and price transparency. But asking 'why not?' invites the reader to give their own reasons for *not* trying it: 'I've never been there before', 'I might not like the choices', and so on. It's a question you don't really want them to answer. You can often drop the 'why not' to make a command that's much stronger.

Finally, there are rhetorical questions, like this famous 1970s slogan for Black Magic® (Rowntree/Nestlé).

Who knows the secret of the Black Magic box?

Obviously, there's no need to answer – 'who knows?' means 'nobody knows'. If questions like this work, they generate mystery and intrigue around the product. If they don't, the answer will probably be 'who cares?'

Explain why

This is a good approach if you need to explain something to the reader before you start selling to them. The headline promises some useful or interesting knowledge, while the body copy goes on to deliver it.

'Why' is powerful because it promises insight as well as information. The reader feels they're going to gain some deeper understanding, instead of just being handed a bunch of facts:

Why your in-office server could soon be a thing of the past.

You probably think of your server as the heart of your office network. But more and more businesses are getting rid of their servers completely. By moving your essential data to the cloud, you can keep it safe and accessible without the hassle and expense of in-house hardware.

As this example shows, it can't hurt to put a little drama into the setup. In reality, on-site servers are still vital to many businesses, and far from being 'a thing of the past'. But the copy needs a bit of spice to draw the reader into a subject that otherwise might not interest them at first glance.

Break the news

The power of a news headline is that it promises readers some information or benefit that they couldn't have had before. That neutralises their reflex to say 'not interested' or 'don't need it'. If what you're offering is truly new, they've got to find out more before they can be sure it's not for them.

Everyone likes novelty. Newness is always more interesting than sameness, unless the reader is 100% happy with what they've got already. And since the grass is always greener, that's pretty unlikely.

On top of that, newness usually means progress, so whatever readers know about the product already, news still promises some extra benefit, even if it's only a slight improvement.

To signal novelty, you can use words like 'new', 'now', 'introducing', 'discover', 'find out about' and so on:

> Now there's a new way to buy a car without setting foot in a showroom.

To make this work, you need to have genuine news to share. You've probably bought a 'new and improved' product, like a washing powder, where you would have been hard pressed to say what had actually changed. If your news isn't really that big a deal, consider whether there's a better way to frame the benefit that doesn't set the reader up for disappointment.

Give a command

Go ahead – use a command. Come right out and tell the reader what to do. Link your aims directly with your copy. Just do it!

Commands are powerful, and they get attention because we don't receive that many simple, direct orders in normal life. Unless you're in uniform, even instructions from superiors at work are usually softened with something like 'Do you think you might be able to…?' or 'Could you just…?'

One of the main ways to use commands in copywriting is in calls to action (see chapter 8). But they can work in headlines too.

Sometimes, the effect is similar to describing a benefit. For example, here's Bellroy's headline promoting its compact wallets:

Slim your wallet

This isn't really telling the reader to do anything, apart from try the product. What the reader takes away is 'buy our stuff and make your wallet slimmer'. But that's still a strong message, and the command gets it across in only three words.

Bellroy gives a simple, clear command to the reader.

A higher-level command could be inspirational, as with Nike's famous slogan challenging its customers to perform better and achieve more:

Just Do It.

However, commands don't have to be confrontational. They can simply encourage the reader to do something they'd already quite like to do, as in this famous slogan for KitKat® (Nestlé):

Have a break, have a KitKat.

A gentler approach is to guide the reader towards a particular state of mind, by talking about something less concrete:

Imagine a life free of financial worry.

TRY THIS

Headline hunt

Check out the headlines in marketing materials you see in the newspaper, on TV, on the sides of buses or anywhere else.

Is it clear who the headline is aimed at? How do you know?

How does the headline work? What reaction is it trying to get from the reader? Does it offer any benefits, and if so, how are they expressed?

7

STRUCTURE YOUR COPY

Put the right points in the right order
and make your copy flow.

Why structure matters

As we've seen, your copy needs to keep the reader reading. That means not only saying the right things, but also saying them in the right order. A good structure lets your argument unfold in the reader's mind in a clear, logical way, never putting a foot wrong. It also makes the reader's experience easier and more enjoyable, so they're more likely to remember your message and act on it.

This chapter suggests a few ways to structure your copy. You can choose one to give shape to your whole project, or combine them by using different approaches for different sections.

Make a plan

Although it may be tempting to jump straight into the writing, you'll probably get a better result in less time if you plan your copy first.

First, jot down all the high-level ideas you want to cover. Each one of these will become a paragraph in your final copy. You can put them on scraps of paper or sticky notes, or just type them into a document. Then, once you've got everything down, move the themes around until they look like they'll link up in a logical way.

Let's go back to the *Wind-O* brief from chapter 5, for a landing page to promote double glazing to homeowners. Our plan for the copy might go something like this:

Headline: talk about a great home improvement that pays for itself

Opening: story of Mr and Mrs H, who used a cowboy window firm and lived to regret it

Why Mr and Mrs H basically had the right idea: improve your home with double glazing and you can get the money back in property value (facts and figures to back this up)

Other benefits: appearance, soundproofing, energy savings

Why you need to watch out for the cowboys

How to pick a good double-glazing firm

How *Wind-O* ticks all the boxes: good product; established firm (number of installations); big on service

What customers say

What will happen when you contact us – surveying, quoting, choosing, installation and after-sales, step by step

Special offer

Call to action – fill in the form to get a quote

This plan features some of the techniques for shaping your copy that we'll look at in this chapter: starting with a story, the AIDA structure, solving a problem, giving the reader information and working through a process step by step.

For longer pieces of writing, you might want to put subheadings in your plan, so you can break it up into broad areas as well as specific themes.

When you're planning, just plan. None of the wording in your plan needs to go into your actual copy. If you get drawn into thinking about words and phrases, write them down somewhere else and bring your attention back to the plan. At this stage, all you're doing is fitting ideas together.

Start strong

Your opening is the second most important part of your copy after the headline, and almost as difficult to get right. It needs to draw the reader in, make them want to keep reading and show you're going to deliver on the promise of your headline. Here are a few ideas.

If you didn't use a question in the headline (see 'Ask a question' in chapter 6), you could use one for your opening. For example:

> What's the one thing holding your company back? For many service businesses, holding on to clients makes the difference between failure and success.

Stories are a great way to start, because readers want to find out what happens next:

> Jim stared at his spreadsheet in disbelief. How had they lost so many clients in so little time? If he was going to show his boss these numbers, he'd better say how he planned to make them right.

As this example shows, you usually create more drama if you start in the middle. Front-loading this copy with tons of background about Jim's job, or what his company does, would turn the reader right off. Your copy will be much more immersive if you throw the reader in at the deep end. (We'll come back to storytelling in chapter 11.)

You can use 'if this then that' to make a direct logical link between the reader's situation and how they want to change it:

> If you own a fast-growing business, you need a sure-fire way to keep clients coming back for more.

Or you can use a metaphor to say the same thing with an arresting image:

> You wouldn't try to fill a bucket if it had a hole. But that's exactly what business owners do when they try to boost revenues without thinking about customer retention.

There's more about metaphors in chapter 9, and more on writing about real-world things (using concrete language) in chapter 11.

Another approach is to bring up something the reader already knows, and link it to something useful you can tell them:

> It's far easier to sell to an existing client than gain a new one. So how can you make sure clients stay with you for the long haul?

We've seen how you need to work with your reader's beliefs rather than undermining them. But you can still say something surprising to get their attention. Look at the opening from George Orwell's *Nineteen Eighty-Four*:

> It was a bright cold day in April, and the clocks were striking thirteen.

This works by meeting some of our expectations while challenging others. The first part puts us in a familiar setting, so there's something for us to hold on to. But the second part shows there's something very different going on. And we want to find out what it is.

You can do the same thing in copy by speaking to the reader's situation but saying something unexpected about it. This suggests that you know something valuable and relevant that they don't (yet). For example:

> The best way to hold on to clients has nothing to do with service, or even pricing.

Write the middle first

As with headlines, it's often easier to leave your opening until later, rather than trying to write it first.

First, nail down the core of your copy, which is usually the part about the benefits of the product. (If you're anything like me, you'll find that your head is full of little details and phrases that you need to get down on paper, in any order, before you organise them.)

Then write your headline, and decide how you'll get the reader from that starting point to the benefits.

Finally, link through to your call action with some persuasive points (which we'll look at in chapter 13).

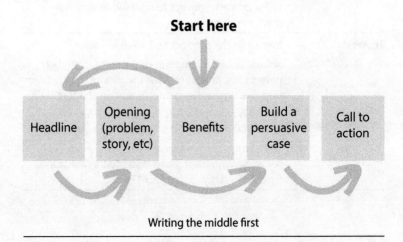

Start here

| Headline | Opening (problem, story, etc) | Benefits | Build a persuasive case | Call to action |

Writing the middle first

You could also write a placeholder opening that you know isn't quite right, in the knowledge that you'll come back and improve it later.

AIDA and her daughters

Google 'copywriting formulas' and you'll find hundreds of ready-made copy plans, each with their own catchy acronym. In fact, there are so many that it *might* be quicker to just write something rather than choose the right one.

No tool is right for every job. You may not want to use formulas every time, or obey them too slavishly. But they can still help you remember what you need to include, or give you a basic structure to build on.

The mother of all copywriting templates is AIDA, which stands for 'Attention, Interest, Desire, Action'. Many other copywriting formulas are broadly similar to AIDA, or simply expand on it. Here are some ideas for how you could use AIDA to structure your copy:

Attention	Write a headline that gets readers' attention and makes them want to read on (chapter 6)
	Tell relevant readers that you're talking to them
	Offer a benefit or the solution to a problem
	Use a creative concept (chapter 9) to generate more interest
Interest	Introduce the product and what it does
	See the reader's situation or problem from their perspective and show how the product helps them (see 'See it from the reader's side' in chapter 11)
	Give the reader the information they need to understand the product or what it does (see below)
	Tell a story – of how the product was made, or of someone who used it and benefited as a result (see 'Tell a story' in chapter 11)

Desire	Describe the benefits (chapter 3) in greater detail to make the reader want the product
	Evoke the experience of using the product (see 'Make it real' in chapter 11)
	Use persuasive techniques (chapter 13) to strengthen the benefits
	Activate social proof by bringing in testimonials, case studies, endorsements or reviews to show that other people are using and benefiting from the product (See 'Social proof' in chapter 13)
Action	Recap the main benefit(s) and/or return to the creative theme
	Use persuasion (chapter 13) to remove obstacles, overcome objections and convince readers that it's OK to act – or point out the negative consequences of *not* acting
	Tell the reader what to do next with a strong, clear call to action (chapter 8)

To be clear, I'm not suggesting you try to do *everything* here in every piece of copy you write. This is more like a menu you can pick from, based on the needs of your project.

Don't let a template twist your copy out of shape. For example, there isn't always a clear boundary between 'interest' and 'desire'. If so, don't repeat yourself just to fit the template. Let your copy be the way it wants.

AIDA works very well for self-contained pieces of copy that take readers all the way from indifference to a purchase, like sales letters or landing pages. But it can help you shape larger-scale projects too. For example, the diagram overleaf shows an online customer journey for a B2B firm that helps other firms stay on top of their obligations under data protection law.

Each piece of content corresponds to a stage of AIDA. First, the LinkedIn ad gets readers' attention by evoking a problem they might have: legal non-compliance. They click through, and their interest is aroused by an ebook written

Attention

LinkedIn ad

Are you up
to speed
with data
protection
law?

Interest

Ebook

Overview
of data
protection law

Why you
need an
expert partner

Desire

Website

Service details

Skills and
experience

Testimonials,
case studies

Clients

Action

Enquiry
End goal

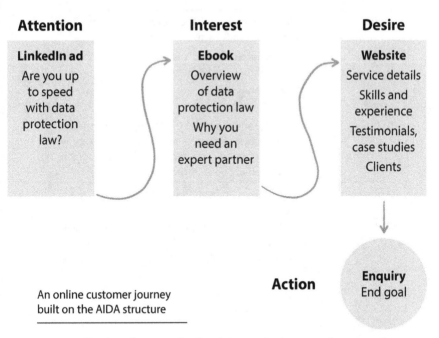

An online customer journey
built on the AIDA structure

especially for them, which ultimately brings them to the firm's website. When they arrive there, the service pages, case studies and customer testimonials make them want to work with the firm, and they get in touch.

Solve a problem

Positioning the product as the solution to a problem is a foolproof way to structure your copy.

You start with a problem (or 'pain point') that's troubling the reader, which you thought about in chapter 4. To keep things simple, it's best to focus on just one problem.

Your headline presents the problem, and maybe mentions a solution. Then the body copy talks about the problem in more detail before explaining exactly how the product solves it.

To put that another way, you take the benefit you want to highlight and combine it with a situation your reader is facing, or something they'd like to change.

Here's an example from an email by Dropbox, the cloud storage platform:

> Nobody likes burying their work in a pile of email attachments. Or constantly wondering whether a client took a look. Headaches like these not only waste time, but also affect how your work comes across.
>
> That's why we're introducing Dropbox Showcase, available today with Dropbox Professional. Showcase lets you share all your work in one professionally branded page...

This targets a specific readership (designers and other creatives) and talks about one of their particular problems (disorganised workflow) before offering a solution to it.

As this example shows, it can be worth 'poking the problem'. Before you offer to solve the problem, you spend some time making it sound really bad, or pointing out implications that the reader may not have thought of (like 'how your work comes across'). Later on, when you've explained your solution, you can return to the same theme by talking about what might happen if the reader doesn't act, or the risks of them carrying on as they are.

You can make the problem/solution more engaging by saying that you've faced the same situation:

> **The one thing I wish I'd known when I started out in business**
>
> I remember when I was working to get my business off the ground, like you are now. It seemed everyone had some sort of advice to give me. How to set up a company. How to choose premises. How to build a website. But the one thing I really wanted to know was how to get the top-quality leads and referrals that would make my business grow.

If you take this approach, you may also need to establish the credibility of the 'writer', so readers believe that they really are speaking from experience. Longer sales letters and landing pages sometimes do this with a section called something like 'Who I am and why you should listen to me'.

Give information

Imagine we're married. It's 7am and we're still in bed. Turning to you, I announce, 'As a busy parent, you can never get enough help around the house.'

Ignoring your puzzled frown, I plough on. 'I believe there's no better way to start the day than a refreshing hot drink delivered right to your bedside.'

You're clearly getting irritated, so I cut to the chase. 'That's why I'm offering to make you a lovely hot cup of tea, right now,' I say.

This silly example illustrates a trap that it's very easy to fall into: telling readers stuff they already know, or don't need to know. You don't need me to tell you that you're busy, or that tea is nice, or that you like it. And you *really* don't care what I believe about tea and when to drink it. You just need to know that I'm going to brew up, and the sooner the better. All that other stuff is wasting your time.

Recall from chapter 1 that different readers are at different points in relation to the bridge you want them to cross. Some have one foot on the bridge already, while others don't even know that it's there. What you tell your reader depends on how much they know right now, and what they need to know before they can decide to buy.

In *Breakthrough Advertising,* Eugene Schwartz describes five stages of awareness that readers pass through on the way to buying a product.[16] As the table shows, your copy has to do more or less depending on which stage they're at.

16 *Breakthrough Advertising* by Eugene M. Schwartz, Bottom Line Books, 2004.

Reader's stage of awareness	What your copy has to do				
	Explain the problem	Link the problem with the reader's situation	Position the product as the solution	Convince the reader to choose the product	Call to action
Completely unaware The reader doesn't know about the product or what it does, or that they have a problem it could solve	●	●	●	●	●
Problem-aware The reader knows they have a problem, but doesn't know there's a solution		●	●	●	●
Solution-aware The reader knows their problem can be solved, but doesn't know that the product can do it			●	●	●
Product-aware The reader knows about the product, but isn't sure about buying it				●	●
Most aware The reader knows all about the product and just wants to know 'the deal'					●

Readers can be in the 'completely unaware' situation when circumstances have changed, or when the product is totally new. For example, suppose the tax authorities have just changed the rules on business expenses, and lots of people will be affected. You're writing an advert for an accountancy firm that can help people stay within the rules. But unless readers know about the new legislation, they won't see any value in the service, or even understand why it exists. So instead of leading with a benefit, you lead with problem awareness:

EH36 will change the way you manage your accounts. Are you ready?

From 1 April 2018, the rules on recording business expenses are changing…

Most copy is aimed at the middle three types of reader: 'problem-aware', 'solution-aware' and 'product-aware'. Copy for 'problem-aware' and 'solution-aware' readers will often take a problem/solution structure: talking about the reader's situation and empathising with them (as we saw in chapter 4) before showing them how things could be different.

A pitfall of writing for 'problem-aware' readers is spending too much time talking about solutions in general, and not enough about the product in particular. As soon as the reader understands that their problem has a solution, start showing them why your product is the *specific* solution they should choose. If you warm up the reader without closing the sale, you're just doing competitors' work for them.

Once the reader moves into the 'product-aware' stage, you switch into convincing them to buy. You can do that by helping them pre-experience the product (which we'll explore in chapter 11) and using persuasive techniques (chapter 13).

If your reader has reached the 'Most aware' stage, your copy doesn't need to do much at all. You just need to tell them to act (see the next chapter) and show them that the buying process is quick and easy. You might also have to deal with 'hygiene factors' like guarantees and returns, or confirm the value of the product or brand with testimonials. If the reader finds out the price of the product at this stage, you may need to present it in a certain way; we'll come back to this in chapter 14 ('Reframe costs').

Take different views

Have you heard the story of the blind men and the elephant? Each of them can reach a different part of the elephant, so each one gets a different idea of what it is. The one holding the tusk says it's a spear; the one feeling the body says it's a wall; the one touching the leg says it's a tree, and so on.

Some products are used in just one way. For example, the way I use a water bottle is probably much the same as the way you use it. Everyone's experience of that product is basically the same. So it's relatively easy to write copy about that one experience.

But it's not always that simple. Some services work by connecting different groups of people, like eBay (buyers and sellers) or Uber (drivers and passengers). Everyone involved uses the same underlying technology platform, but they do it in very different ways.

Or it might be that people have the same experience of a product, but buy it for different reasons, or to get different benefits. Think about a basic feature phone, or 'dumbphone'. For users who don't like learning how to use technology, its key benefit is simplicity. But for parents looking for a phone they can safely give their kids and easily replace if it gets lost, the benefits are durability and affordability.

If you're writing for different user groups who have different experiences of the product, and get different

83

benefits from it, your copy may have to speak to each group separately. That might translate into different website pages for different people ('For drivers', 'For passengers'), or even whole campaigns targeting different groups ('Become a driver', 'Download our app').

It's not only tech products that have multiple dimensions like this. As we saw in chapter 3, the person who buys the product isn't always the person who uses it, and they each have different priorities. Here's how Robinsons (Britvic) introduces its Fruit Shoot range of children's drinks:

> Made using real fruit juice and water, our range of No Added Sugar drinks are a great option to help keep kids refreshed when running, jumping, playing and exploring every day.

Since we're hearing about 'kids' being refreshed (not 'you'), we know the copy is aimed at parents. But that changes when we reach the individual product descriptions:

> Shower your taste buds in sunshine with Orange No Added Sugar. An all-time favourite flavour.

Now the 'you' is the actual consumer – the child – and it's all about the taste.

Or you could take a humorous look at the different ways people use a product. After Eight® (Nestlé), the brand of thin mints, ran a TV ad featuring 'The Gerbil' (nibbling), 'The Wolf' (devouring) and 'The Hawk' (spotting the last mint in the box). More recently, Andrex® (Kimberley-Clark) asked people if they were 'scrunchers' or 'folders' of toilet paper. If it's done well, this approach gives people a new way to see a product through the lens of their own character. But as these two examples also show, some product experiences are better conversation-starters than others.

Another possibility is that everyone uses the product the same way, but different readers are at different stages of awareness (as we saw in the previous section). In that situation, you might want to write different sections or pages for different people, and make sure readers can find the one they need. For example, a site selling video cameras could include a guide for first-time buyers, as well as feature comparison tables for more seasoned users.

Family tree

This is a simple, reliable way to give your copy a strong structure, particularly if you've got a lot of things to cover. You start with the central point, then move on to the others, in descending order of importance. The result is a 'family tree' of points, with each 'parent' point having its own 'children'. The diagram overleaf shows an example.

This is the structure used by newspaper articles, which are all about getting information across as efficiently as possible. The main message is right there in the headline, not buried halfway down the page. That means that even if readers don't make it to the end – or even if they only read the headline – they still take away the central point.

Sketching out your family tree like this gives you a ready-made structure and running order for your copy. For example, if you were writing a web page, you could start with a headline on the main theme, then write a short introductory paragraph to cover the next level down, and finally use multiple short sections with informative headings to mop up the detail at the lowest level. To stop your copy fizzling out on a minor point, you could close with a strong restatement of the main benefit combined with a call to action (see chapter 8).

Sometimes, certain things have to be covered before others. For example, if you want to talk about a bike being cheaper than a car, it makes sense to introduce it as an alternative mode of transport first. The reader has to accept the transport benefit before they'll consider the cost one.

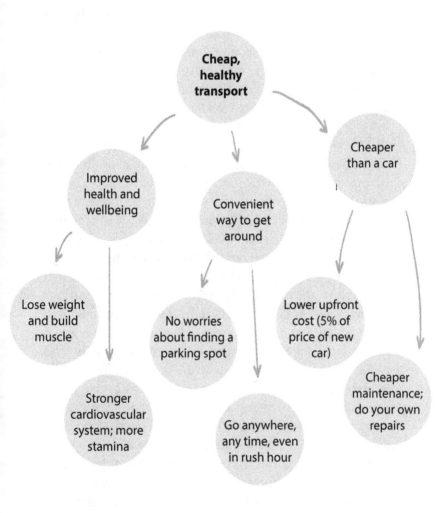

Family tree of some of the benefits of owning a bicycle

Another important factor is where the copy will appear, and who your reader is (chapter 4). If your copy is destined for a health magazine, you'll probably deal with the health benefits first, because those are the ones readers are most likely to be interested in.

Make a list

You've probably seen dozens of clickbait listicles with titles like 'Seven celebs who'll never work in Hollywood again – #3 will shock you!' They've turned numbered lists into a cliché, and a disreputable one at that. But this is still a good way to organise your copy if you've got lots of things to say that are all equally important.

Let's say you're writing about a food processor that does lots of different things. All the functions are equally useful; it's the *range* of options that offers a benefit. You need to get that across without your copy turning into a catalogue of features linked together with 'and' or 'also'.

You could start off with a headline like this:

> Five ways the *MultiChop* helps you make delicious meals in minutes

Then you'd go on to explain the five most important functions and how they'd replace manual tasks like chopping, grating and so on, each one under its own numbered subheading. For a display ad, you could arrange them around an illustration of the *MultiChop*, with lines pointing to different parts of the machine.

One advantage of the numbered list is upfront transparency. The headline tells the reader exactly what they're going to get, and they can then work through all your points, always knowing where they are in the series, or just pick out the bits they want.

Our minds are more like calculators than computers: we can only hold a certain number of things in our 'working memory' at any one time. Cognitive psychologist George A. Miller discovered that the 'magic number' is seven, plus or minus two.[17] So five things should be relatively easy to

---

17 'The Magical Number Seven, Plus or Minus Two: Some Limits on Our Capacity for Processing Information' by George A. Miller, *Psychological Review*, 1956.

remember, seven is OK and nine is pushing it. Go any further than that and you risk the reader forgetting something or getting mixed up.

Go step by step

The best way to tackle a big task is to break it down into smaller chunks. And it's exactly the same when you need to explain a large or complex subject.

With the 'step by step' structure, you work through the steps of a sequence or process and explain each one in turn, as if you were writing recipe instructions.

'Step by step' is ideal if you need the reader to understand something a bit complicated before they can commit to a sale. Suppose you're promoting a conveyancing service. For first-time buyers, the home-buying process is completely new and fairly baffling. What they need is a step-by-step guide to buying a home, showing how conveyancing fits into the bigger picture.

The brand that provides a guide like this can build authority, show empathy with readers and gain their trust. What's more, readers will be able to visualise the buying process in advance, so it's less daunting when they go through it for real (see 'Make it real' in chapter 11).

Another use of 'step by step' is to explain how customers will buy and use a product over a relatively long period, or how benefits will unfold into the future. It's particularly useful for telling B2B prospects how a service will fit with the way they manage their businesses.

Using *ShopData*, step by step

First, we talk to you to find out how you use research data now, and suggest some new approaches you may not have thought of. Then, based on what you tell us, we draw on our 500+ customer panels to gather data on your products and what consumers really think of them. Finally, we present the results to you – in a tailored report, or face to face during your quarterly planning meeting, or both.

B2B buyers are concerned with the costs and benefits of an outsourced service, but they're also worried about the opportunity costs of procuring and implementing it. In other words, they might have to put a lot of time and effort into choosing a new service and getting up to speed with it, and that can make them want to stick with what they have. 'Step by step' maps out the whole process in advance, showing them that each step is easy in itself and also that the overall journey is not that long or demanding.

It's easy to see how this structure lends itself to graphics like timelines or flowcharts. If you're creating an infographic to be shared online, a 'step by step' description is a sure-fire winner – right up there with a pie chart.

However, 'step by step' isn't just for complicated ideas. You can also use it to add movement and interest to descriptions that would otherwise be static:

> First, we take a crunchy biscuit. Then we add a layer of gorgeously gooey caramel. And then we wrap it all up in deliciously chunky choc.

This is much more interesting than 'biscuit and caramel coated in chocolate'. Instead of being ingredients that just get stuck together, the three elements become chapters in a mini-story.

The magic of three

Let's linger in the sweet shop for a moment. If you're a UK reader of a certain age, you might recall this famous slogan for Mars® bars:

> A Mars a day helps you work and play

No, that's not right – as you can probably tell, even if you're too young to remember. The real slogan was:

A Mars a day helps you work, rest and play

This three-part version is much better – even though 'rest' doesn't add much extra meaning, and the two-part one is shorter and simpler. That's because writing structures with three parts are nearly always more satisfying than those with two, four or other numbers.

Here's an example from Glasgow Women's Library:

Safeguarding the history of your grandmothers.
Hearing the memories of your mothers.
Providing inspiration for your daughters.

Mentioning all three generations is far more pleasing than any two of them would have been on their own.

The same applies to the number of sentences in a paragraph. This paragraph follows the rule, to show you what I mean. Three sentences are just right for developing your argument without boring or losing your audience.

Often, the three sentences form logical steps in an argument. First you assert a premise. Then you qualify or develop it. Finally, you take it to its conclusion:

You know you need to sort out your pension. But understanding all those regulations can be difficult, if not impossible. What you really need is a knowledgeable guide.

Or you can make a relevant observation, link it to a benefit and then back it up with a proof point:

Nobody likes being paid late. Our invoice factoring service takes away the hassle, so you can concentrate on real work. So far, we've collected an impressive 85% of the debts we've taken on.

The only problem with the rule of three is when it becomes too much of a rule. It's a great go-to approach because it always gives you a tight, readable structure. But if it gets *too* tight, it can turn into a straitjacket. For example, what if you want to add a fourth point to a paragraph, like I'm doing now? Or a fifth?

Also, threes can get boring. Mix them up with something short.

Rules are for the observance of fools and the instruction of the wise. You use them as long as they're useful, but drop them if they're not. If your copy naturally falls into a three-part structure, that's great. But if you find yourself bending over backwards just to respect the rule, it's time to loosen up.

Use visuals and formats

If you've got a lot to say, bear in mind that the best way to present it might not be a simple block of text. Here are some other techniques you can use:[18]

Use this...	...to communicate this
Subheadings	Key points you want the reader to take away
	Different themes within long copy
	Transitions between one idea and the next
Bold within body copy	Important points or ideas
	Can work as 'sub-subheadings', allowing skim-readers to pick out different themes
Lede or standfirst (block of text in bold at the start of body copy)	Summary of the rest of the copy, and/or teasers and tasters to generate intrigue
PS (additional copy included after the signature of a letter)	Restate key benefits, special offer and/or call to action

18 For a deeper discussion of how visuals, particularly drawings, can help you communicate, see *The Back of the Napkin: Solving Problems and Selling Ideas with Pictures* by Dan Roam, Marshall Cavendish Business, 2009.

Use this...	...to communicate this
Bullet points	Sets of similar items where the number and order aren't that important (such as a list of benefits or features)
Numbered list	Sets of similar items where you want to emphasise how many there are
	Items in rank order (for example, a 'top five')
Table (like this one)	Lists with two or more sets of related items
Diagram with captions and leader lines	Related parts within a system or structure
Flowchart	Sequences, processes or linked decisions
Timeline	Events, stories or histories
Bar chart	Numbers compared with each other
Line graph	Numbers changing over time
Pie chart	Proportions compared with each other (a few large proportions works best)
Family tree	Hierarchy
	Relationships between things or people over time
Venn diagram	Categories with items common to more than one
Emojis	Simple objects, emotions, ideas or stories
Speech bubbles	Dialogue between two people
SMS (text message) conversation	

Readers tend to skim over body copy and latch on to things that stand out visually. You can take advantage of that by including important messages in them. For example, the caption for a product image could mention a benefit, rather than being a straightforward description.

TRY THIS

Restructure it

Next time you're reading a longer piece of copy, like a magazine ad or a sales letter, think about how it could have been structured differently. Could the ideas or information have been arranged in a clearer way?

8
CALLS TO ACTION

Round off your copy and get the reader
to act with a powerful call to action.

What are calls to action?

Calls to action are short sentences that tell the reader to
do something.

In chapter 4, you decided your aim – what you want
your reader to know, feel or do. Calls to action focus on the
'doing' part. For the reader, they're the gateway from active
to passive: from reading, listening or learning to actually
doing something in the real world. You've made your case,
and now it's time for them to take action. As we've seen, that
action could be buying a product, but it could also be just
getting in touch with the company, or something different
like making a donation.

Calls to action normally appear at the end of your
copy, wherever that may be: written at the bottom of
ads, sales letters and articles, or spoken at the end of
broadcast ads. In printed media, they're often marked out
visually in some way. That tells readers that the call to action
is different from the rest of the copy, and that they need to
act on it.

Things are slightly different online. Here, many calls to action are links, so the reader responds simply by clicking on them. The text of the link should describe what will happen when the reader clicks it. For example, it should say something like 'Read our white paper on Agile development', not just 'Click here'. If there are lots of different elements to a web page, readers may not read everything in order, so calls to action are often placed in a sidebar or a header to make sure people don't miss them.

Strong calls to action can be powerful, but they're not 'get out of jail free' cards. They won't magically spur the reader into action if you haven't build up a strong case in the rest of your copy. Your call to action should be a gentle nudge that encourages the reader to do something they're pretty much ready to do.

Basic calls to action

The simplest calls to action tell the reader what to do. They take the form of commands, which are forceful and direct, as we saw in chapter 6 on headlines. They can be vanilla:

Request your free sample now

They can be relaxed...

Pop in any time for a quick demo

...or forceful...

This time-limited offer must end on Sunday.
Act now.

...or enthusiastic, like this from Netflix's online ads:

Get watching

Basic calls to action are usually short, so they're a good choice for situations where space is tight and readers are easily distracted, as in many online ads.

Bring in benefits and persuasion

For something more engaging, you can build in a benefit. This turns the call to action into an offer of a deal – 'do this and you'll get that':

> To start earning this unbeatable rate of interest, open your account today.

It's best to use a benefit you've already described, rather than introduce a new one in the call to action. By this point, you're aiming to close the sale, not make your case.

You can also strengthen your call to action with a persuasive angle, which we'll explore in detail in chapter 13. For example, you can use scarcity to tell the reader that they need to act quickly or lose out:

> Remember, you only have 30 days to renew your subscription at this one-time-only discount. Call us today to secure your saving.

Or you could use social proof to emphasise that others are already enjoying the benefits of the product:

> To join thousands of happy *Vaxxo* customers, order yours now from Amazon and other major online stores.

Keep it simple

Whatever you ask the reader to do, keep it as simple as you can. Give it as few stages as possible – ideally, just one. If readers have to do more than one thing, bring the elements together so the reader understands exactly what they need to do, and in what order:

> To renew your licence, fill in this form, then bring it to any Post Office along with your old licence, a passport photo and the £25 fee.

Your project might include more than one call to action – on the different elements of a mailshot, for example, or on the different pages of a website. You might well feel that it's worth varying the length and phrasing, rather than using exactly the same words over and over. That's fine, as long as the reader never gets confused over what they should be doing next.

If readers have a choice about what to do, make sure you give all the options every time – or, if space is short, use a generic phrase that covers all of them (like 'Get in touch with us today'). Mentioning one option on its own might make people wonder whether the others will work too.

Show that it's quick and easy

Readers need to understand that whatever you're asking them to do is quick and easy. They don't want to put too much effort into it, and they don't want to have to think, or make a lot of decisions. If they're doing something new, they want to know what they're getting into before they start.

Even if your reader completely agrees with what you're saying, you're still asking them to make a change, however small. And most people resist change rather than embracing it, even when the change would benefit them. If you want the reader to cross the bridge we saw in chapter 1, you need to remove all the obstacles in their way.

Here are a few examples:

What you want the reader to do	What you want them to think about it	What you could write
Fill in and return a paper form	Won't take long Won't cost anything	To get your sample, take five minutes to fill in the form below and send it to us. You don't need a stamp.

What you want the reader to do	What you want them to think about it	What you could write
Fill in an online form	Won't take long Won't be confusing	To request a callback, complete this simple one-page form. The labels on the right explain what you need to enter in each box.
Make a phone call	Won't be awkward Won't lead to cold calls	To get a free, no-obligation quote, call our friendly sales team on 01234 123456. We'll never call you unless you ask us to.
Go to a branch	Won't have to travel very far Won't take too long	Drop into one of our 47 branches nationwide for your 10-minute design consultation.
Go to a supermarket and find a product	Will be in stock and easy to find Won't slow down my weekly shop	You can find *Cheese-O* in the dairy section at all major supermarkets.
Discuss needs, request a proposal (B2B)	Won't take too much management time and effort	We're always happy to discuss your needs and offer advice on the right setup for your business.

We'll look at more ways to overcome readers' objections in chapter 13.

Stepping stones

Sometimes, you might want to guide readers to the next stage of their journey, or encourage them to read on, rather than ask for the sale. For example, here's some copy for the outside of a direct mailing envelope.

Open now to save up to 60% on your car insurance...

Obviously, this isn't the whole story. The reader knows they'll have to do more than just open the envelope to get that saving. This is just a way to connect the action they need to take *now* with the benefit they'll receive in the end.

In B2B particularly, there are times when you need to start by giving the reader information, or building up your credibility. You can use different bits of content, linked by calls to action, to take the reader through these stepping stones to a sale. (This sequence is sometimes called the 'sales funnel' or 'customer journey', and the steps along the way are sometimes called 'touchpoints'.) The diagram shows how the stages in the data-protection example from chapter 7 (in 'AIDA and her daughters') could be linked by calls to action.

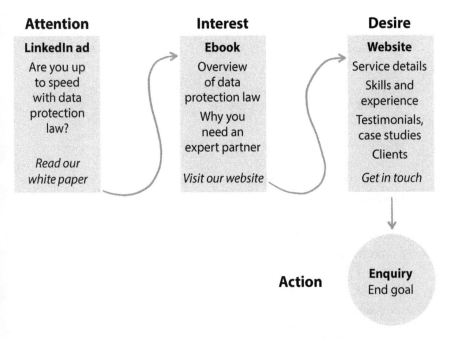

Stepping stones, linked by calls to action, bringing B2B prospects from first interest through information and on to making an enquiry

As with other types of call to action, it's important to be clear on what you're asking the reader to do, and what they'll get in return, at each step. Each call to action should promise some sort of value, and the stage that it leads to should deliver on that promise. Also, it's probably best if each call to action only refers to the next stepping stone, rather than jumping ahead to what the reader might do later on.

Another way to use stepping stones is to guide readers through the pages or sections of a website in a particular order. For example, at the end of a page, you could write:

> Now read more about <u>our approach</u> or <u>get in touch</u>
> to talk through your project.

Many visitors will ignore this and go wherever they want, but that's OK. It still plants the idea that they should continue browsing the site, and it's a more positive ending than just tailing off at the end of the content.

TRY THIS

Call yourself to action

What are you going to do next, when you stop reading this book? How will it benefit you? Think up a call to action to encourage yourself to do it.

PART THREE
IMPROVE YOUR COPY

9
GET **CREATIVE**

Twenty proven ways to make your copy
more original, witty or emotive.

What is creativity, and why do you need it?

Telling the reader about benefits is the heart of
copywriting. It should always be the first thing you try,
and sometimes you may not need to do much more. But at
other times, you need something more powerful. You need
a splash of creativity.

You know creativity when you see it. But how would you
define it? What does creative copywriting actually mean?

In my view, there are three sides to the answer.

The first is being *original*. Creative copy is different from
what's around it, or from what people expect. That means
readers notice and remember it, where a bland 'me too'
message would just get ignored or forgotten. All else being
equal, we remember things that stand out, not those that
blend in.

Original copy achieves what leading copywriter Steve
Harrison calls 'relevant abruption'.[19] It gets in the reader's face

19 *How to Do Better Creative Work* by Steve Harrison, Pearson Education, 2009.

with an eye-catching message that they weren't necessarily looking for, but now realise they might be interested in.

The second side is being *witty*: saying something in a clever, interesting or unexpected way. Thoughtful copy makes readers think, too. They see something subtle, intriguing or clever, and that makes them 'lean in' to find out more.

Wit often means making your message less obvious, but more interesting. It's about taking something that's easy to say, or something that's been said many times before, and making it fresh and new. As novelist Joy Williams puts it, it's about 'unexpressing the expressible' – saying something by not saying it.[20]

Witty copy offers readers a deal. Instead of being passively spoon-fed a message, they've got to pay active attention and do a little bit of brainwork. In return, they get a double payoff: the meaning of the copy and the satisfaction of having worked it out. In the title of a famous book, they get 'a smile in the mind'.[21]

Originality grabs attention, but wit earns respect. Because you invite the reader to work with you on creating meaning, they feel that you and they are on the same level. You didn't talk down to them, and they responded by engaging with your ideas. Now you're equal partners who share an understanding.

Witty doesn't necessarily mean funny. A witty idea might make the reader laugh, but it might just make them smile, nod in recognition or stop and think. On the other hand, some things can be funny without being particularly witty, like slapstick comedy or LOLcat videos. You can still use them, but they might not involve the reader or earn their respect in quite the same way.

---

20 See the interview at tinyurl.com/unexpress
21 *A Smile in the Mind: Witty Thinking in Graphic Design* by Beryl McAlhone, David Stuart, Greg Quinton and Nick Asbury, Phaidon, 2016.

Finally, creative copy is *emotive*. It makes the reader feel something. That feeling could be something pleasant, like fun, excitement, aspiration, security or confidence. It could be something deep, like love, mystery or compassion. Or it could even be something negative, like fear or anxiety.

The emotion your copy evokes could be one that the reader already feels, as we saw in chapter 4. For example, many ads for baby products appeal strongly to parents' love for their children. Or you could aim to make the reader feel something new, like charity ads do by introducing a good cause and making people care about it.

The stronger the reader's emotions, the more likely they are to take your message on board and remember it. They may also associate their feelings with the product, which is why you should be careful about arousing negative emotions.

Originality, wit and emotion are all matters of degree; you can dial them up or down. You can be conservative, mildly original or radically leftfield. You can say it straight, drop in a subtle wordplay or turn an entire ad into a riddle. You can be cold and detached, add a little human interest or go full-on tearjerker. And you can do all these things in different combinations.

Creativity with purpose

At its very best, marketing can tell powerful truths and enrich our culture – *almost* like art. And the best copywriting can hold a mirror to our lives and loves – *almost* like literature. But they can never be *quite* the same, because while art is complete in itself, marketing always has an ulterior motive, whether it admits it or not. Unlike Monet, marketing is not content just to paint you a beautiful bridge. It has to tempt you across it too.

So although creative copywriting may be very original, witty or emotive, it isn't any of those things for their own

Be original
Make the reader notice and remember

Be witty
Make the reader think

Be emotive
Make the reader feel

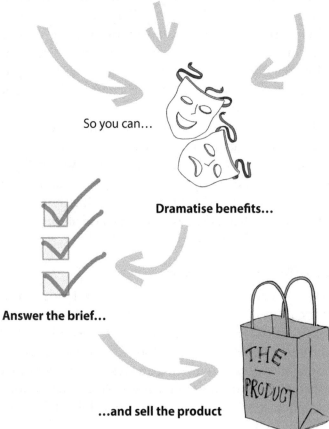

So you can…

Dramatise benefits…

Answer the brief…

…and sell the product

What your creative copywriting needs to do

sake. It's about solving a problem in a creative way. If it has any artistic merit, this will be because it rises to that challenge particularly well.

Remember, copywriting is writing with a job to do. And when it comes to being creative, your job has three parts: to *dramatise benefits, answer the brief* and *sell the product.*

Dramatising benefits means bringing them to life and making them as striking and colourful as you can. The examples in this chapter will show you what that might mean.

Answering the brief means sticking to the plan you made in chapter 5, so you target the right reader and dramatise the right benefits, and work within the constraints of the project.

Lastly, selling the product means exactly what it says. However good your creative idea is, it's still got to be about the product. If you get carried away with your creativity, your copy may be very original, witty or emotive, but it could be selling itself rather than the product.

Bob Levenson, one of the original 'Mad Men' of 1960s Manhattan, suggested a simple test for this. 'If you look at an ad and fall in love with the brilliance of it, try taking the product out of it,' he said. 'If you still love the ad, it's no good. Don't make your ad interesting; make your product interesting.'

To sum up this chapter so far: creativity means making your copy original, witty or emotive so you can dramatise benefits, answer the brief and sell the product.

Some starting points for creative copy

Creative thinking is a fuzzy, intuitive process that everyone has to learn for themselves, and it's hard to write instructions that will work every time. Here, I'm going to suggest 20 starting points to help you find your own way.[22]

22 For more insights on creativity, read *Hey Whipple, Squeeze This!* by Luke Sullivan, John Wiley, 2016, and *One Plus One Equals Three* by Dave Trott, Pan Macmillan, 2016.

Many of the examples here are headlines from print adverts, but that's only because they make nice snappy quotes. It's up to you how you use the ideas. For short projects, like adverts, they could shape the whole of your copy. For longer pieces of writing, you might want to use them for individual sections. And of course, you can adapt or combine them however you want.

Start simple

As a first step, just reword the brief as a value proposition addressed to your reader. For now, don't try to make it original, witty or emotional. Don't worry about the writing style either. Just put it on paper as simply as you can.

For example:

> *Malus Maximus* is a dry cider that tastes really good and is made here in the UK, just with organic ingredients.
>
> It's sort of a cider equivalent of craft ale – quite strong, with a distinctive taste and hipster branding.
>
> You should try it, which you can do by buying it at some supermarkets or online and drinking it at home.

Starting simple has two big advantages. First, you get something down on paper and conquer the blank page. Before, you had nothing, but now you're already into the process of refining and sharpening. If you find editing easier than writing, like I do, that's a big step forward.

Second, you can start with the essentials and add whatever else you need, rather than starting with something convoluted and trying to unpick it. Pitch your tent in the middle of your message, then strike out for somewhere more adventurous – if you need to.

Mix it up

Steve Jobs said, 'Creativity is just connecting things.' He meant that 'new' ideas are never completely new: they're just new *combinations* of things that already exist.

In his book *A Technique for Producing Ideas*, James Webb Young suggests that strong advertising ideas often come from combining specific knowledge about the product and its users on one hand, and general knowledge of other things on the other. To have good ideas, you need to gather lots of information, 'chew it over' and let your subconscious mind make new connections.[23]

In chapter 2, we saw how important it is to learn all you can about the product. But to make new combinations, you need to 'know a little about a lot' – not just the product. So it's a good idea to read, watch and listen to many different things, including those you're not necessarily interested in yourself. (This sort of cultural grazing is much easier now we have digital treasure troves like Wikipedia, YouTube, Brain Pickings,[24] Farnam Street[25] and 99% Invisible.[26])

See it differently

Seeing the product from another angle can suggest different, more powerful ways to write about it. For example:

- **Repurpose it.** How else could you use the product? What would a child do with it? What does it look like, and what could it be mistaken for?
- **Distort it.** What would the product be like if it was squashed, stretched, short, tall, fat, thin, tiny, enormous? What if it was small enough to fit in your pocket, or so big that it filled the room? What if it was made of modelling clay, or cheese, or paper, or gold?

23 *A Technique for Producing Ideas* by James Webb Young, Stellar Editions, 2016.
24 See brainpickings.org
25 See farnamstreetblog.com
26 See 99percentinvisible.org

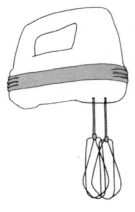 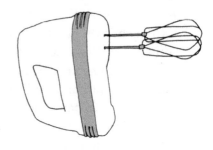

Handy kitchen appliance   Chef's secret weapon

Play around with different ways of seeing to discover new creative directions

- **Displace it.** What would the product be like if it was under the sea, on the Moon, in the jungle, in a cartoon, in a videogame, in the past, in the future? How would it be in the world of *Harry Potter*, *Wonder Woman*, *The Hunger Games*, *The Lord of the Rings* or *Breaking Bad*?

Working this way might seem too frivolous, too playful. But as developmental psychologist Jean Piaget said, 'Play is the answer to how anything new comes about.' In other words, to play is to create.

When we play, there's no goal to reach, no product to deliver. So it's OK to fail. In fact, if there is no goal, you *can't* fail. When you think like that, it's easier to improvise, explore the unknown and see things in new ways.

The ideas you come up with might not be usable as they are. They might not be usable at all. But they still might suggest new directions to explore – directions you might never have found if you'd stayed on more predictable paths.[27]

27 For a treasure trove of fascinating perspectives to fuel your creativity, see *The Art of Looking Sideways* by Alan Fletcher, Phaidon, 2001.

Find a metaphor

A metaphor is thinking about one thing as if it was something else, so you can understand or explain it better. (Closely related are similes, which say that one thing is *like* another, and analogies, which draw parallels between two things.)

Metaphors are like the combinations we saw in the previous section put into words. Robert Frost said, 'An idea is a feat of association, and the height of it is a good metaphor.'

Metaphors aren't exact comparisons. They highlight some attributes and hide others. When we say that a good friend has been 'a rock', we don't mean that they've been cold, hard and rooted to the spot. We mean they've been solid and dependable.

In the same way, you can use a metaphor to link the product with something else that the reader knows, in order to highlight certain benefits. For example:

Is your body due for an MOT?[28]

If you're a man over 40, you're at greater risk of lots of health problems – some big, some small. Book a health check with your GP and make sure you stay on the road long into retirement.

Physically, a human body doesn't have much in common with a car. But there is one common theme: both health problems and breakdowns can be avoided through monitoring and 'maintenance'.

This metaphor makes a link from something the audience might be interested in (motoring) to something they might be trying to avoid (their health). The parallel between the two appeals to consistency (see chapter 13): you look after your car, so why not do the same for your body? You could

28   The MOT is a UK government test to make sure a car is still roadworthy.

easily turn it into a visual too – for example, a car owner being examined beside his car, or a 'service due' warning light appearing when he looks in the bathroom mirror.

Staying with motoring, here's the slogan for Castrol GTX engine oil:

Liquid engineering

This elegant two-word metaphor equates the humble oil with a sophisticated professional skill. While motorists might find it hard to visualise oil lubricating the hidden insides of their engine, they can certainly picture an attentive mechanic tuning it up. The metaphor takes something obscure and abstract and makes it visible and concrete.

Metaphors can help to make new things more familiar, like the bridge in chapter 1 that introduced copywriting. When automobiles were first invented, people called them 'horseless carriages' to express something they didn't know in terms of what they did. We still use 'wireless' to describe connections that haven't used wires for years.

For example, here's the tagline for Pedigree® Dentastix® (Mars®), the healthy treat for dogs:

You brush, they chomp.

This draws an analogy between dogs and their owners to suggest that Dentastix® are 'the toothbrush for dogs'.

Metaphors can also make undesirable things more attractive, or boring things more colourful. This slogan is by Habito, a service to help people apply for a mortgage:

We'll eat your mortgage broccoli.

The parallel between making a mortgage application and eating your broccoli works on multiple levels. They're both 'good for you' in different ways, but they're also both duties that you might avoid or put off. (The line assumes you don't like broccoli, but the meaning is still clear even if you do, thanks to broccoli's bad reputation.) The offer to eat the broccoli recalls a friendly offer in the school dining hall to take something off your plate that you'd rather not deal with. And all in five words – that's the power of metaphor.

The same approach works just as well in B2B, as in this slogan for Hootsuite®, the social media management platform:

Less haystack. More needle.

This turns an abstract process (generating new-business leads) into something concrete and tangible, while expressing a benefit (more high-value leads for less effort).

Metaphors can also work the other way round, by making familiar things new and exciting – like the famous Guinness 'Surfers' ad.[29] It starts from two metaphors: Guinness froth as white wave-caps ('white horses'), and Guinness drinkers waiting for their pints to settle as surfers waiting for the perfect wave. Then it develops those ideas through some truly beautiful words and images, resulting in one of the greatest ads of all time.

Waves as white horses in the stunning Guinness 'Surfers' ad.
REPRODUCED BY KIND PERMISSION OF GUINNESS

29 Watch it at tinyurl.com/guinness-surfers

At the other end of the scale, bear in mind that certain metaphors have become clichés. It's often because they're good ways to illustrate particular abstract concepts, or services that are hard to depict in an interesting way. For example, you may have seen ads using images of padlocks for online security, umbrellas for insurance, light bulbs for new ideas, chess pieces for strategy or signposts for planning.[30] If visual metaphors like these have become commonplace in the area you're writing about, you might stand out more with some simple, literal copy that *doesn't* use a metaphor.

Draw a contrast

While comparisons highlight similarities, contrasts highlight differences. Instead of saying 'this is like that', they say 'this is different from that', or 'this, but on the other hand that'. Contrast copy usually expresses some sort of tension between two things, while resolving them into one rounded, balanced message.

To explore contrasts, think about how you could highlight the differences between benefits, or different aspects of the same benefit. For example, here's the tagline for the Vauxhall Corsa:

The small car with the big personality

Here, the contrast is between the size of the car and its 'personality' – which really means its styling, design and accessories, as well as the intangible values of the Corsa brand. So it's a way to say you get a lot of car for your money.

This contrast covers several benefits (and shortcomings) at once. If the reader is interested in a small car, it says that the Corsa has more character than its rivals. If the reader sees small size as a disadvantage, it suggests that other benefits could outweigh that – it may be compact, but it's cool.

30 You can find a comprehensive list at tinyurl.com/101cliches

As this example shows, the two things that you contrast don't have to be *exact* opposites. In the Corsa line, 'big' and 'small' suggest a direct contrast because they have opposite meanings. But when you look closer, they're really just two ideas that the copy brings together to make a point.

Actually, if the opposition is *too* direct, you might end up with a contradiction rather than a contrast. For example, have a look at this portmanteau slogan for the Toyota Yaris:

Bigsmall.

I think this is less successful, because everyone knows something can't be big and small at the same time – unless it's the TARDIS. So instead of being intriguing, the line just ends up sounding illogical.

The right sentence structure and word choice can make your contrast more vivid, as in this slogan created by Saatchi & Saatchi in the 1970s for the Health Education Council.

Everybody likes a drink. Nobody likes a drunk.

Here, the link is strengthened by the opposition of 'everybody' and 'nobody' and the alliteration of 'drink' and 'drunk', while the contrasting meanings of those words (good time, bad behaviour) hammer home the message. (We'll come back to alliteration in chapter 12.)

Make 'em laugh

Humour is a powerful weapon for the copywriter. It gets readers' attention, which is hard. It sticks in their memory, which is even harder. It makes them like you, which can be persuasive (as we'll see in chapter 13). And most importantly, it can express benefits in a very powerful way – as long as it's relevant to the product.

Some firms might worry that being funny makes their product look silly or trivial. But humour can still make a serious point. In 1984, Walter Mondale won the Democratic

117

nomination by borrowing restaurant chain Wendy's famous slogan 'Where's the beef?' to undermine the flimsy proposals of his rival, Gary Hart. What started out as a throwaway gag in a TV spot has passed into the language as a metaphor for anything insubstantial or weak.

There are lots of ways to be funny. You can play it straight or get surreal. You can use broad strokes or subtle wit. You can be rude or refined. You can be sincere or sarcastic. It all depends on how the product or brand should talk. As we'll see later in this chapter, the nudge-wink gag of a hot snack sounds very different from the elegant wordplay of a bank. (There's more about this in chapter 15, on tone of voice.)

Whatever approach you choose, it obviously has to be funny. However, that doesn't mean you should necessarily laugh at it yourself. In fact, that could even be a danger sign. When it comes to writing copy, funny means *funny to the reader* – not necessarily to you or the client. While some readers may love *Monty Python*, others might be more into *Mrs Brown's Boys*.

One way to find a humorous angle is to take some aspect of the product, then exaggerate or twist it until it becomes funny. Award-winning copywriter Paul Burke suggests starting with the seven deadly sins – pride, greed, lust, envy, gluttony, wrath and sloth – and applying them to the product to see where that leads.[31]

For example, Money Supermarket's marketing, with the line 'You're so Money Supermarket', takes the pride of the bargain-hunter to ludicrous lengths. Kellogg's TV ads for Crunchy Nut Corn Flakes® showed people getting into various amusing predicaments because they were so greedy for the product, with this tagline:

The trouble is they taste too good.

31 'No laughing matter: why advertising isn't funny anymore' by Paul Burke, *Campaign*, 11 May 2017.

A lot of comedy is based on *Schadenfreude*. When we see someone slip up, ideally due to some fault of their own, we feel glad that we're not them. Some copy gets laughs at the expense of someone who doesn't use the product, like the ads showing the misfortunes of those who 'Should've gone to Specsavers'. Apple's 'Get a Mac' campaign drew contrasts between an uptight 'PC' character and a laid-back 'Mac' to gently poke fun at the rival platform. Ads like this make readers want to avoid becoming the butt of the joke, which they do by buying the product.

Certain subjects, like death and suffering, are probably off-limits for humour. You wouldn't crack gags during a eulogy at a funeral, or wave a £5 note under the nose of a homeless person. And some jokes don't travel across national boundaries very well, because they depend on readers recognising a particular situation, experience or cultural reference.

Finally, let your humour speak for itself. Imagine you meet a man at a party who immediately claims to have a great sense of humour. You probably won't believe him – in fact, you're more likely to think the exact opposite. If he really wants to convince you, what he needs to do is tell a really good joke. In the same way, funny copy should simply be funny, without self-consciousness or overselling the gag.

Play on words

If you're going for humour, lots of your first ideas will be puns around the brand or product name – the creative equivalent of spur-of-the-moment wisecracks. Unfortunately, they may not have that much power to communicate. Wordplay isn't necessarily wit.

For example, at my local swimming pool, sponsored messages from local firms flash up on the electronic scoreboard. They usually say things like 'move into the fast lane' or 'dive into our new menu'. So all they really do is make a superficial link between the reader's situation (swimming) and the product. They don't express any benefit, or generate any intrigue, or make people want to learn more. What's more, they're not even that funny. In terms of the ideas pool, they're definitely at the shallow end.

Compare that with the inspired slogan for *Cocktail*, the 1988 film starring Tom Cruise:

When he pours, he reigns.

This works on several levels. First, it keys into readers' attention by echoing a phrase they already know ('it never rains but it pours'), but makes it different enough to be more than just a recycled cliché. Then it uses a play on words to confirm the setting of the film ('pouring' = barkeeping) and the premise of the story ('reigns' = a really talented barman).

The lesson: only make a pun to make a point. A pun without an idea is just a throwaway gag. But a pun that actually says something can be expressive, memorable and incredibly concise – as well as fun.

For example, Tesco uses this slogan on its delivery vans (alongside a picture of some juicy tomatoes):

Freshly clicked.

This isn't just a joke; it's a message. By evoking the phrase 'freshly picked', Tesco draws a parallel between picking tomatoes off the vine, picking them out in the supermarket and clicking to buy them online. That addresses readers' concerns about being lumped with second-rate or out-of-date produce when they shop online.

Staying with grocery vans, here's a line used by Abel & Cole, who deliver fresh veg:

Fields on wheels

This twists the familiar expression 'meals on wheels' to express how Abel & Cole bring produce from the field to your door.

Timberland used a pun to express a fairly complex benefit with its headline:

> Paint the colour on our shoes?
> We'd rather dye.

The first part informs readers that shoe colour can in fact be painted on, which they may never have considered. The literal meaning of the second half ('dye') explains that Timberland uses dye instead, while the underlying meaning ('rather die') gets across the superiority of dye over paint, as well as a principled commitment to quality. But while it's taken me over 50 words to explain all that literally, the puntastic copy does the same job with nine.

Another option is to make a pun on the product or brand name itself, as Dave Trott did with these taglines emphasising product durability:

> Ariston and on and on

And social desirability:

> Hello Tosh, got a Toshiba?

More recently, Cillit Bang (Reckitt Benckiser), the cleaning range, uses its name as the basis for a strong benefit-based tagline:

> Bang! And the dirt is gone.

Puns on names are rarely used these days, maybe because people take their brands a bit more seriously than they used to. (Cillit Bang's campaign is knowingly retro.) But they can be a great way to embed a name in a memorable phrase, avoiding the problem of people remembering the tagline but forgetting who it was for.

Even if your pun ideas aren't deep enough to work as headlines or concepts, you should still write them down. You might still be able to use them somewhere – for example, in the body copy of an ad.

Use images

Lots of copywriters are wordy types who are happy to leave layout and images to visually minded designers. But some of the strongest copy depends on visuals for its impact, if not its actual meaning. In fact, some 'copy' has no words at all – it's just an idea made visible.

A good rule of thumb is to put meaning into either words or pictures, but not both at once. In other words, copy and imagery should work together to convey a single idea. There's no need for the copy to describe what people can see in the image, and there's no need for the image to show what the copy says.

Let's say you're writing an ad for a new bicycle cleaning fluid. Your target readers are cycling enthusiasts, and the benefit of the product is a quick, easy way to clean every part of their bike. If you were writing the headline with no imagery in mind, you might go for something like:

Show your bike how much you love it.

However, if your ad can include a picture of a gleaming bicycle, you can take out 'bike', since the image is now saying that for you:

Show it some love.

The final step is an image showing a cyclist leaning a cheek lovingly on the bike's front tyre, with the cleaning product in the foreground. Here, you can get away with no copy at all, if you and the client are brave enough.

What if the product is a B2B service that you can't really depict? You could try showing the customers of the service, or the people who deliver it. You could use a synecdoche: a smaller part that stands for the whole, like a duster for a cleaning service. Or you could use a visual metaphor for a benefit, as long as it isn't clichéd.

Decisions about design and imagery have a big influence on how your copy works, so it's best to get involved in them if you can. That's why advertising agencies use two-person creative teams comprising a copywriter and an art director. They bounce ideas off each other, looking at the brief from their different but complementary perspectives. If you have the chance to work with a designer this way, take it. It's really refreshing to work with someone who thinks differently.

If that sort of partnership isn't possible, you'll need to find another method of explaining your image ideas to the designer. While some designers will take the time to read and digest your copy, others will just dive right in and attack the brief from a visual angle – which is their job, after all. If you can talk to them directly, that's great. If not, you can try putting notes explaining your ideas in your copy document. Or you could draw a rough sketch (called a 'scamp') to show how you imagine copy, images and layout working together.

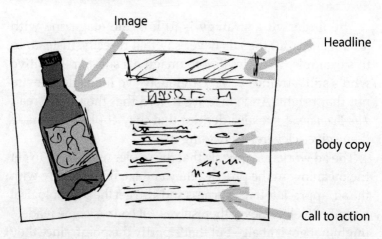

Draw a scamp to show how your copy could work with layout and imagery

Show, don't tell

When you watch a TV drama or a play, the characters rarely say exactly what they mean. Instead, you have to read between the lines, or interpret their actions, to work out what they're thinking. That makes the drama more convincing, and the experience of watching it more rewarding.

When you show rather than tell, you involve the reader in creating the message for themselves, rather than just giving them information about the product, or telling them to buy it. Instead of sitting back and passively receiving the message, the reader has to join the dots for themselves. For example:

> **ingle ells,**
> **ingle ells.**
>
> The holidays aren't the same without JB.

The famous copy-only ads for *The Economist*, originally created by David Abbott, are brilliant examples of this.

> **'I never read The Economist'**
>
> – Management trainee. Aged 42.

The underlying strategy is to link the magazine with intelligence. But the ads never say that directly. Instead, in this example, we're invited to imagine a sub-par executive who's still a trainee at 42. Obviously, we infer that they're not that bright. And since we're told that they don't read *The Economist*, we also deduce that they could have made themselves cleverer by reading it.

The ad works as a puzzle that the reader must solve to get the meaning. In the process, they engage more deeply with the ad, appreciate its cleverness and also get the psychological payoff of feeling clever themselves. Of course, some readers might not get it at all – but that's partly the point, since they probably wouldn't buy the magazine anyway.

'Show, don't tell' also applies to copy that depends on imagery. A later *Economist* poster featured just the signature red background and a picture of Brains, the geeky character from *Thunderbirds*. You had to know who Brains was to get the joke, but that was part of the appeal.

Ford did something similar with its old campaign promoting its convertible cars. The design featured a picture of an old-fashioned pram alongside this headline.

The only convertible that outsells Ford.

To get this line, the reader had to see that convertibles are like prams because they both have hoods that pull back. Then they had to work out that there are (or were) more prams in the world than convertibles. This led them to the point: Ford's convertibles were the top seller.

You could even use the structure of language itself to make your point. SwissLife did this with its ads promoting life insurance:

You are the only woman I love a man now.

For all life's twists and turns:
Flexible financial plans.

The headline is formed by overlapping two sentences hinging on a common phrase (in this case, 'I love'). But although the two sentences share a concept (here, loving someone), they have completely different meanings. The copy expresses the idea that 'life comes at you fast', while our experience of reading it conveys the feeling of disorientation when that happens. (Unlike *The Economist*, SwissLife gives readers a little clue to the puzzle with the phrase 'twists and turns'.)

The interesting thing about 'show, don't tell' is that it often places obstacles in the reader's way. The reader has to put a bit of thought in, and if they don't, they may never

You are the only woman I love a man now.

For all life's twists and turns:
Flexible financial plans.

SwissLife uses sentence structure to make its point.

understand the message. That can make clients nervous that the copy simply won't connect with readers, which will mean their marketing spend goes to waste. But the reader is far more likely to remember a message that they've helped to create. Provided it's done well, 'show, don't tell' trades immediacy for impact.

Stir it up

Provocative copy can shock the reader, shake them out of complacency and make them want to read on. Here's some copy for Harrison's Fund, a charity fighting Duchenne Muscular Dystrophy (DMD) that does exactly that:

I wish my son had cancer

Harrison, my 6 year old, has Duchenne Muscular Dystrophy. He's one of 2,500 sufferers in the UK who'll die from it, most before they're 20. Unlike cancer, there's no cure and no treatment. And because you've never heard of it, very little funding either. My only hope is to raise as much money as possible for the research scientists. They're close to a major breakthrough. Your £5 can get them even closer.

The headline is so outrageous that you've *got* to find out why someone would say such an extraordinary thing, and that carries you through the rest of the copy.[32]

Another approach is to be divisive: pleasing some readers while irritating or even offending others. That's fine, as long as you only alienate readers who would never buy the product. For example, check out this slogan for Calpol® (Johnson & Johnson), the children's medicine:

32 You can read more about the campaign at tinyurl.com/wishmyson

I WISH MY SON HAD CANCER

Harrison, my 6 year old, has Duchenne Muscular Dystrophy. He's one of 2,500 sufferers in the UK who'll die from it, most before they're 20. Unlike cancer, there's no cure and no treatment. And because you've never heard of it, very little funding either. My only hope is to raise as much money as possible for the research scientists. They're close to a major breakthrough. Your £5 can get them even closer.

Help stop Duchenne for good. Text MAKE12 £5 to 70070. Or go to harrisonsfund.com

Confrontational copywriting from Harrison's Fund. REPRODUCED BY KIND PERMISSION OF HARRISON'S FUND (WWW.HARRISONSFUND.ORG)

If you've got kids, you'll understand

For parents, it's a knowing reference to a shared experience that no one can really appreciate until they go through it. If you don't have children, it's infuriatingly smug and a massive turn-off. But that's OK, because non-parents will never buy Calpol – not even as a gift. The slogan doesn't lose anything by annoying them.

Pot Noodle (Unilever) used something a bit spicier for its campaign in 2002:

The slag of all snacks

Here, the idea is divisive, but so is the language. Using the offensive insult 'slag'[33] earned Pot Noodle a ban on its TV ads following complaints – along with some publicity that was arguably more valuable than the ad alone could ever have been. Of course, the brand could never be certain that would happen in advance. Stirring it up is a high-risk, high-return proposition where you gamble a bit of reputation in the hope of winning attention.

Do different

'Do different' was the original motto of the University of East Anglia. When my dad arrived to run the university's PR in the 1960s, he wanted its student prospectus to live up to those words.

At that time, nearly all higher education prospectuses came in standard sizes, usually A5 (about 6" by 8"). So my dad decided to make UEA's perfectly square. Now it stood out, quite literally, on the shelf. It felt different, it looked different and it echoed the boxy, brutalist architecture of the UEA campus. The medium was the message: this was no humdrum provincial college; it was a trailblazer.

---

33   The closest US equivalent is the equally offensive 'skank'.

The lesson is clear: if everyone else is zigging, you zag.

To be different is to be memorable. All else being equal, people will remember you better if you stand out from the crowd. Psychologists call this the Von Restorff effect.

Since the financial crisis of 2007, financial services brands have emphasised their softer side, positioning themselves as faithful friends rather than mere moneymen. Swiss private bankers Hyposwiss broke from the norm with a range of copy-only ads mocking the earnest self-importance of top finance brands. Here are a few of their headlines:

"We are not more than just a bank."

"It's not about you and us. It's about your money."

"Time is time. Money is money."

"If you look at a risk in a positive way, it is still a risk."

The ads were rounded off with a tagline that summed up the attitude of the campaign with a subversion of a clichéd phrase:

Expect the expected.

Hyposwiss's copy stood out in a landscape of over-friendly financial brands. But by suggesting that banking should be 'all business', it also made other banks seem vain and flaky in comparison. It wasn't just that Hyposwiss looked better – they made their rivals look worse.[34]

Do the opposite

A great way to discover new creative directions is to do the opposite of what people normally do when writing about your product. First, you think of things that are obvious or

34 For more on outwitting the competition (in copywriting and elsewhere), see *Predatory Thinking* by Dave Trott, Pan Macmillan, 2013.

taken for granted about your brief. Then you ask, 'What if we did the opposite?'

Top copywriter Nick Asbury uses the example of an annual report.[35] Normally, annual reports are long, dry, factual and blandly positive in their tone. But what if they were short, like a poem or a picture book? What if they were written like a romance, or a graphic novel? What if they lied, or told jokes, or wandered off the point? What if they were doleful, or wistful, or fanciful?

Not every idea you come up with will be workable, but this is an easy way to generate lots of different avenues to explore. From there, you can choose the most promising ones and start writing.

A good example of 'oppositional thinking' is Harvey Nichols' 'Sorry, I spent it on myself' Christmas campaign. It featured people giving their relatives outrageously cheap gifts because they'd blown all their cash treating themselves.[36] Instead of talking about giving, like every other seasonal ad, Harvey Nichols talked about greed and selfishness. That made other brands look pious or twee, helping Harvey Nichols stand out at a time when brands compete most fiercely for customers' attention.

Reframe it

Reframing means looking at the same thing in a different way.

A Labrador can be a cuddly friend to a child, or a trusted guide to a blind person. A knife can be an artistic tool when wielded by a chef, but a deadly weapon in the hands of a psychopath.

35 'How to write an award-winning* annual report' by Nick Asbury, *Creative Review*, 6 September 2016.
36 Watch the ad at tinyurl.com/sorryspent. The cheapo gifts really existed and were available to buy.

Sometimes, companies can get locked into thinking about themselves in a certain way. Over time, they develop fixed ideas about why people buy their products, or what they like about them. And that's a problem if your job is to think of new angles for their marketing.

In chapter 3, we looked at identifying the most important benefit(s) you want to talk about. But if it turns out those benefits don't really lead to any creative ideas, you might do better with a different, less 'important' benefit.

In the very first episode of *Mad Men*, Don Draper attends a creative meeting with executives from Lucky Strike. The ideas soon dry up, so Don just asks the suits to chat about how their cigarettes are made. When they mention that the tobacco is 'grown, cut, cured and toasted', Don pounces on the new Lucky Strike slogan:

It's Toasted.

In fact, *all* cigarettes have toasted tobacco, so 'toasted' wasn't really a benefit at all, just a generic feature. But Don could still use it to reframe the product from a health risk to something comforting and warm, like a home-cooked meal. ('It's Toasted' really was a Lucky Strike slogan.)

Check out this headline from a leaflet by Dor-2-Dor, a leaflet marketing firm, that dropped through my letterbox:

Keep Fit and Get Paid

Reliable adult leaflet deliverers wanted

You don't see many benefits in recruitment ads; most firms seem to feel the offer of work is enough. You'd definitely expect that approach with a casual, low-skilled job like leaflet delivery, but instead Dor-2-Dor reframes it as an opportunity to improve your health and get paid for it – a fantastic proposition, particularly just after Christmas, when this leaflet went out.

Give it a twist

Humour is a great way to reframe. Taking a different view can help you dramatise a benefit and give people a laugh of recognition at the same time. The joke and the benefit are woven together, so if the reader remembers one, they should also remember the other.

Flowers bring colour and scent to summertime, but their pollen makes hay-fever sufferers' lives a misery. So Benadryl® (Johnson & Johnson) reframed the blooms as hardened criminals terrorising the innocent, and their own allergy treatment as the tough justice they deserved:

> Flowers. Don't let them get away with it.

There isn't much about the actual benefits of the product, yet the copy still works brilliantly. By trading information for entertainment, Benadryl® stood out in a market filled with generic medicines making generic claims.

IKEA®'s TV ad for bedroom furniture took a different angle on something we don't consciously think about very much:

> The moment has come. There can be no hesitation. You've gotta go do what you prepared to do. There will be those that try and stop you. Let 'em try. This is your hour. Now take it. Because tonight, you're gonna fight 'til you can't fight no more.
>
> Win at sleeping.

Again, the copy doesn't talk about the benefits of IKEA®'s furniture directly. Instead, it homes in on what the reader is really concerned about – a good night's sleep – and turns it from simple inactivity into something they might want to take more care over. From there, the idea of choosing good bedroom furniture follows just as naturally as night follows day.

Switch perspectives

Most copy is written either as if the brand itself is talking, or in a sort of omniscient 'voice of God'. But sometimes it's better to write it from someone else's perspective.

The most obvious voice to bring in is that of customers, who are more likely to be honest about a brand and its products. That's the idea behind featuring customer testimonials on websites. Some of these quotes can be a bit dull and worthy, but this ad from Edinburgh accountants Cowan & Partners offers a nice twist on the formula:

> **"Three words to describe my accountants?**
> **Better than me at numbers."**
>
> Joe Tree, Rocket, Newhaven Road
> A Cowan & Partners client for 15 years

Apart from the humour, which makes the quote far more memorable, this also captures the relief of finding a trusted expert who'll take away your worries.

As we saw in chapter 3, buyers aren't always users, and in some cases the user's view of the product might be more persuasive. For example, back in the 1980s, cat food Whiskas® (Mars®) used this tagline:

> Cats would buy Whiskas

More recently, here's a great ad for Lego® that takes the same approach in a more intriguing way:

> A red submarine was sailing on the streets of Marrakesh when it spotted a Minotaur shooting samurai swords, aliens and Machu Picchus at an army of gruesome hunters, and at that moment a Hero Factory robot stopped Napoleon and the Astronaut from crossing the labyrinth on its five legged camel, which made the entire Circus mad and made the lion, the race

car number 7 and the Coliseum quickly climb Mount Everest looking for a pot full of pirate ships that would save the day and get rid of The Cannibal, the magic Christmas Tree and the Terrible Chocolate Monster.

This brilliantly evokes the way children play, bringing in anything and everything from the environment or their own imaginations. To write it from the perspective of the brand, or even a parent, would be hopelessly patronising and uncool. We need to hear this tumbling cavalcade of characters from the mouth of its creator.

This poster from UNISON, the UK public-sector union, offers a new perspective on those who deliver social care:

I couldn't cope without my care worker	**I can't cope with being a care worker**
Margaret, recovering from hip operation	Alysha, home care worker

Your public services are in crisis.
Get involved at publicservicechampions.org

UNISON's hard-hitting poster presents two very different views of the same reality. REPRODUCED BY KIND PERMISSION OF UNISON/GOOD AGENCY

The parallel structure, hinging on the word 'cope', invites the reader to give care workers' needs the same weight as their own.

Another approach is to bring in the perspective of someone who seems more distant from the product, but can still talk about a benefit of it. Here's an example from the University of San Francisco:

> For the rest of your life, every job interview will begin with your potential employer saying: "Oh, I love San Francisco!"

This could easily have been something like 'Come and study in beautiful San Fran'. But using the words of the future interviewer puts a completely different angle on the choice of university, framing it as a decision with lifelong consequences far beyond enjoying a few years at college.

Another angle would be to take the view of someone who envies users of the product, or regrets buying a rival product, or has just decided to switch to the product. The copy might work well as a story written from their perspective (see 'Tell a story' in chapter 11).

You might even want to take the view of someone who the product *doesn't* help. For example, an intruder alarm offers security and peace of mind to homeowners. A straightforward benefits-based approach would be something like:

> Protect what matters most with the *HomeGuard* 3000.

However, alarms also make life difficult for burglars. You could use this to take a problem/solution angle using fear:

> Burglars are out there.
> Let's keep it that way.

Or even humour:

Burglary's an easy life.
Don't make it any easier.

Finally, you could pretend that your copy is for someone else, when actually it's aimed at the reader, like this sign by the Forest Preserves of Cook County:

Attention Deer!

<u>Do not</u> eat the human food

It is hard to digest and doesn't
provide the nutrients you need

It decays your teeth
(good luck finding a deer dentist)

It teaches you to approach all humans for food

It assists the spread of diseases
that can kill you and your friends

This is totally unexpected, uses humour to make a serious point and piques the reader's curiosity – because we all like reading things that aren't meant for us.

Turn weakness into strength

If you're struggling to find that one key benefit or USP to hang your copy on, you could try turning a 'so what?' aspect of the product into a benefit, possibly throwing some shade at competitors in the process.

Avis®, the car-hire firm, did just that with its famous slogan:

We try harder.

Hertz® was the market leader at the time, and Avis® was in second place. While choosing the market leader can be very reassuring to customers, choosing second place might just feel like second best. Avis® turned that on its head by suggesting that the market leader might be complacent, while the runner-up had something to prove – and that meant better service.

Stella Artois (AB Inbev), the European lager, pulled a similar trick with its slogan:

Reassuringly expensive.

Costing more than competitors is a liability, unless you can persuade people that higher price denotes higher quality. Stella Artois did that and more, implying that beer drinkers might actually *seek out* a pricier pint because it gave them a 'reassurance' of quality.

This email copy from JustGiving takes a similar approach:

Download your fundraising poster

In the lonely pre-Facebook days, many fundraisers used a traditional technique known as 'putting up a poster' to share news of their upcoming event or activity.

Go on – be retro

The pedantic, history-textbook tone, spiced up with sarcasm, turns the poster from an old-fashioned irrelevance into almost a hipster choice. The copy encourages the reader to look past their objection and see the fun of a hands-on activity.

Get meta

Have you watched the US TV series *Mr. Robot*? Elliot, the main character, often addresses you directly, putting you in the position of a silent observer inside his mind. Whatever conspiracy Elliot is caught up in, you're definitely complicit.

Hello, friend.
"Hello, friend?" That's lame.
Maybe I should give you a name.
But that's a slippery slope.
You're only in my head.

This is called 'breaking the fourth wall' – instead of passively watching the drama, you're drawn right into it, making you feel almost like a character yourself. You can do something similar by making your copy refer to itself, or talking about the reader's experience of reading it. This text from the outside of a TV Licensing envelope uses the physical letter to make a point about switching to electronic billing:

> Make this your last paper licence
> at tvlicensing.co.uk/update

This exploits the reader's negative feelings to make a positive point. Don't like brown envelopes on the doormat, sorting out paperwork or wasting trees? Go digital and do something about it.

Here's a long-copy ad by the British Heart Foundation that takes a similar approach, but with much more emotional punch:

> **It's a toss-up between reading this and one of those insurance adverts.**
>
> You know, the kind with all of the waffle about lowest ever, low rates. Anything to take your mind off the journey. To speed things along until you get home. But what if you never make it home? Because heart disease can kill when you least expect it. Even now. Right here, in front of this poster. Without any kind of warning at all. Now there's a thought that's hard to come to terms with. But while you're reading

> this, research is happening. And with research there
> is hope. Together we can beat heart disease. Join
> the fight at bhf.org.uk and help us fight for every
> heartbeat. So which ad next, online dating agency
> or low rate broadband?

This gets attention by pointing out things that the reader probably wasn't consciously aware of: the poster they're looking at, the others around it, the journey ahead, their own heartbeat and the research that's going on. The overall effect is to place the reader firmly in their own personal here-and-now and make them think about big issues like life, death and time, and the choices they have available.

If you use this sort of technique, remember your creative mission. If you can be meta in a way that dramatises benefits, meets the brief and sells the product, all well and good. But if you do it for its own sake, or too self-consciously, you'll just come across as smug and self-satisfied.

Borrow interest

Spin-off series, celebrity endorsements, musical collaborations... they all work by taking people's enthusiasm for one thing and pulling it across to something else.

Marketers call this 'borrowed interest'. In a way, it's not the most creative technique, because you're just piggybacking your message on to something else so you can smuggle it into the reader's brain. But it all depends on how it's done.

Sticking your product next to some random famous thing probably won't work. The reader will just start thinking how much they like that other thing, and forget yours. But if there's a reason for the association, you've got a much better chance of holding their interest.

When insurance group Norwich Union changed its name to Aviva, it ran a TV ad featuring celebrities who'd changed their names before finding fame: Ringo Starr (born

Richard Starkey), Alice Cooper (Vincent Furnier), Bruce Willis (Walter Willis) and so on. The ad had formidable star power, but it was all there for a reason.

If your client can't afford Bruce Willis, there may still be a way to allude to borrowed interest without angering any lawyers. Here's part of an ad I wrote for HelloFresh, a firm that offers regular deliveries of fresh produce along with recipe suggestions:

Master cheffing.

Ever felt you could be up there wowing the judges, if only you had the time?

At HelloFresh, we do all the hard work for you, so all you have to do is whip up the dish and bask in the glory...

Here, the idea was to gently remind readers about a TV programme they'd probably seen (*MasterChef*), then use their possible response to it ('I wish I could cook like that!') to promote the product.

Hiscox, the insurance firm, took a similar approach with this ad:

Every Maverick needs a Goose

We assign a single, dedicated claims handler as standard to help every claim fly through smoothly.

The headline is brilliantly intriguing, and the 'fly through' gives a nice link back to *Top Gun* (and geese). However, both depend on the audience knowing a film that could have come out 13 years before they were born. That's what makes borrowed interest a double-edged sword: if people don't get the reference, your copy might sound meaningless or downright weird.

Be agile

Agile marketing is borrowing interest at the speed of light. It's about hitching your message to current news items or cultural events, using what readers are already thinking and talking about to drive home your marketing message.

Agile marketing has really come into its own with the advent of social media, where creative ideas can be thought up, written, designed and posted in a matter of hours – which they need to be, or people will have moved on to the next story. You'll also need a client who has the social presence and open-mindedness to make an agile campaign possible.

At the 2017 Oscars, *La La Land* was wrongly announced as the winner of Best Picture, before the mistake was corrected to *Moonlight*. Many advertisers were quick to jump on the resulting furore, but I think the best response was the 12-second text-only video Asda posted on Twitter:[37]

Asda jumps on the 2017 Oscars mix-up

37 See the tweet at tinyurl.com/asdatweet

And the award for quality food retailer of the year
goes to…
Marks and Spencer.
Sorry, wrong card.
Asda!
Awkward.

In the 2017 presidential election in France, centrist
Emmanuel Macron defeated far-right candidate Marine Le
Pen, prompting this riposte from airline Royal Jordanian:[38]

France is not that far… right?

Royal Jordanian trolls Marine Le Pen during
the 2017 French presidential election

38 See the tweet at tinyurl.com/royaljordanian

As with plays on words, these ideas worked because they made a real link between the event and the brand. They weren't just topical jokes that anyone could make; they could only come from the brand, or at least one like it. Asda linked two mix-ups between plausible award winners, while Royal Jordanian brought together politics and international travel.

At the other end of the scale are the uninspired 'Valentine's Day offers' that clog up your inbox every February. Not only do they have no real link with the occasion they're trying to ride on, they also take the same approach as many others, practically guaranteeing that they won't stand out. If everyone jumps on the same bandwagon, the wheels will probably fall off.

See what others did

If you genuinely can't think of a new idea, there's always the option of borrowing one from somewhere else. I don't mean straight-out plagiarism, but rather using other people's good ideas as a starting point for your own.

Many copywriters maintain a 'swipe file' of examples that they like, which they consult when the ideas just won't flow. There are plenty of books and websites on the same theme.[39] It's amazing how often just looking at the solutions other copywriters have found gives you new ideas of your own.

If you do decide to 'borrow' an idea, look further than your own doorstep. If you look at ads from a particular sector (cars, finance) you'll often see very clear trends, because rival brands tend to imitate each other's ideas. Shake that up by taking a style or approach from a completely unrelated industry and imagining how it could work for your brief.

---

39 For a compilation of excellent copy, with commentary from the copywriters themselves, get *The Copy Book: How some of the best advertising writers in the world write their advertising*, Taschen, 2011. For an online collection of annotated ads and sales letters, visit Swipe-Worthy at swiped.co. Pinterest is another good place to browse curated copy examples.

Take it further

Your creative ideas might be part of a bigger picture. If you're working for an agency, they'll probably be looking for more than one idea, so they can create a campaign rather than a single ad. Or, if you're working for the client direct, they might really like your idea and ask for more – even if your brief is only to come up with one.

Either way, you need to think about how you can come up with more ideas on the same theme, or that work in the same way. Some ideas are very strong in themselves, but they're one of a kind, so any follow-up ends up looking weak. But an idea that can be repeated over and over, with each new version adding something new, is copywriting gold. It can be like how John Peel described The Fall: 'always different, always the same'.

Apply your creativity

Pick an object you can see right now and think of a creative way to sell it, using one of the ideas in this chapter. How could you compare it, contrast it, picture it, reframe it, make it controversial, make it funny or turn its weakness into strength?

10
FIND YOUR **FLOW**

Every copywriter gets stuck sometimes.
Here are some ideas for getting moving again.

Just think

When you're under pressure to write something, it's only natural to focus on the output: the words you need to come up with. But just as important is the *input*: the things, ideas and connections that go into your writing. If you don't have the right ingredients, you can't make the finished dish.

To put that another way: copywriting is really copy*thinking*. The actual writing is just capturing the results of that process.

So give yourself the chance to think. Get away from your computer, your laptop, your notepad or whatever else you use to write. Get away from distractions too, like your TV, phone or tablet. Go to a quiet space and just think about the brief for ten minutes, without even trying to write anything down.

This is a good approach if you're a very wordy copywriter who likes tinkering with sentences and phrases to get them just so. That's a good talent to have, but when you're looking for ideas, it can tie you up in details when you need to see the big picture. If a big brush is all you have, broad strokes are all you can paint.

Switch it up

Not finding good ideas where you are? Try moving somewhere else. That could mean physically, mentally or both.

One simple technique is just to change venue. Instead of sitting and staring at a screen with gritted teeth, take yourself off somewhere else with a pen and paper. Different sights, sounds, feelings and smells prompt different thoughts. The new venue could be a room in your house, an office breakout space, a café, a park or anywhere.

Different environment, different ideas. PHOTO: ENGIN AKYURT AT PIXABAY

Another approach is to give your brain some different food. If you sit with a brief for too long, you can get sucked into a spiral of recycling the same thoughts and ideas. Break it up by reading, watching or listening to something completely different. If you're writing about fruit juice, watch some sci-fi. If you're selling yoga courses, listen to some thrash metal. When you come back to the brief, you might find some new ideas waiting for you.

Free your writing

Free writing is a useful technique if you're feeling really stuck for ideas and just can't move forward. It's a sort of personal brainstorming session.

All you have to do is write (or type) continuously for a set period – say three minutes. You can write about the product, or your experience of trying to write about the product, or just whatever comes into your head at that moment. It really doesn't matter what comes out. Just keep writing.

Free writing can help to remove mental blocks and let ideas surface from your unconscious mind. It stops you slipping into editing rather than writing, or improving rather than creating. Some writers do a quick burst every morning, as a sort of 'warm-up' for the day's writing.

Engage your unconscious

Have you ever tried and tried to remember the name of an actor or a song, only for it to pop into your head later, when you were thinking about something else?

Your unconscious mind can solve a lot of problems for you. But it works in its own way, and at its own pace.

That's the problem with techniques like brainstorming. Yes, the teamwork and random connections can throw up interesting new angles. But you're still toiling in an ideas factory, churning out the concepts under time pressure (and peer pressure).

The simplest way to engage your unconscious is just to sleep. Let the problem sink into your mind overnight and see what surfaces in the morning. Keep a pen and paper by your bed just in case.

Since your body and mind are two halves of one whole, physical activity can help too. Go for a walk, a run, a swim or whatever you enjoy. Meditate, if that's your thing. Different movements for your body often lead to different thoughts in your mind.

Work through weaker ideas

As the saying goes, 'Success lies on the far side of failure'. Remember, the good ideas are out there – and sometimes, finding them is a question of moving past the bad ones. The more you can get down on paper, the quicker that process will be.

To take the pressure off completely, you can even focus on having *bad* ideas. Go ahead and write down the worst approaches you can think of, just to get them out of the way. You might be surprised at what comes after them.

As Thomas Edison said, 'I haven't failed. I've just found 10,000 ways that won't work.'

The power of 'yes' and 'no'

Ideas are fragile. Once they're born, they need to be cared for. And they can easily be crushed if someone stamps on them before they've had a chance to grow.

'Yes, and…' is a great technique for developing ideas. Basically, you're only allowed to accept what someone has said and expand on it by responding, 'Yes, and…'. Questioning or shutting down ideas is against the rules, so each idea gets picked up and taken as far as it can go.

Comedians use 'Yes, and…' when they're improvising, to keep their sketch moving forward. The technique is also used in creative brainstorms and business meetings, to encourage people to collaborate and share ideas.

'Yes, and…' is obviously useful when you're working with other people. But you might also need to use it internally, particularly if you have a tendency to self-criticise. 'Yes, and…' is about suspending your disbelief. It gives you the time and space to think ideas through and see their true worth before you start to judge them.

The quickest way to kill an idea is just to say 'no'. But as top creative Gideon Amichay explains, not every 'no' is the same. Sometimes 'no' is actually 'no, comma' –

'No, we don't have the budget', or 'No, there isn't time', or 'No, try something else'. This kind of 'no' can motivate us to try harder, or challenge us to take a new direction. 'Resistance is good,' says Gideon. 'Resistance in innovation, in hi-tech, in art, etc. is great… NO is the beginning of a YES.'[40]

You might hear 'no' from your client, an account handler, a creative director or a colleague you share your work with. Or you might hear it from your own inner voice. If so, find the 'no, comma'. Why is this idea wrong? Why won't it work? How does it need to change, or what else needs to change, to make it work? (There's more on responding to feedback in chapter 16.)

---

40 *No, No, No, No, No, Yes: Insights From a Creative Journey* by Gideon Amichay. No, No, No, No, No, Yes LLC, 2014.

11

ENGAGE YOUR READER

Draw your reader in by talking about real life
with everyday words, or telling them a story.

What is engagement?

When digital marketers talk about 'engagement', they
sometimes mean getting people to do certain things online,
like sharing or liking on social media. But I'm talking about
something much broader than that.

When you write engaging copy, you hold a conversation
with your reader. You talk to them as an equal – just one
person telling another about something they might like. You
use their language, but without talking down. You respect
their intelligence. You appreciate that they're probably busy,
bored or tired, and you remember that they probably didn't
ask for your message. Basically, you treat your reader as
you'd like to be treated yourself.

Talk to your reader

Marketing is a 'one to many' form of communication, and
your copy will be read by lots of people (we hope). But it's
still good to think of your reader as an individual person
rather than a group. Some of the best copy works like a

conversation between writer and reader. On the other hand, some of the worst copy has the impersonal feel of a one-way communication, like a memo from managers to the workforce.

Check out this bit of copy promoting gym membership.

> Members of *Flex Gym* can make use of a wide range of equipment, including treadmills, steppers and free weights. Regular use of the gym can bring many health benefits, including improved fitness and weight loss, often in a matter of weeks.

It gets the point across, but it's a bit dull. Now here's the same thing, said a different way.

> When you join our gym, you'll be able to use all our equipment, from treadmills and steppers to free weights. Visit us regularly and you could get fitter, leaner and healthier within just a few weeks.

The literal meaning of both these is exactly the same, but the second version talks to the reader directly, using 'you' three times, while the first doesn't use it at all. The second one also uses 'our', setting up a relationship between the gym and the reader, and paints a picture of what the reader will do in the future ('join our gym', 'visit us regularly', 'get fitter, leaner and healthier').

Addressing the reader is one of the easiest yet most powerful ways to make your copy engaging. Instead of talking about something 'over there' in a neutral way, you're talking to the reader directly, one to one. That pulls them into your copy, involving them more deeply in what you're saying, as if you really were having a conversation.

Most readers will be alone when they read your copy, so address them as an individual, not part of a group. Even if you're targeting a specific demographic, don't say 'Hey, anglers!' or 'Calling all audiophiles' or anything similar. It shatters the sense of a one-on-one conversation.

Don't write for the client

As you work on your copy, it's easy to slip from talking to your reader into writing for your client (or an agency creative director or account handler working on their behalf). After all, they commissioned the copy, they'll be the first to read it and they may have the authority to approve or reject it. Obviously, you want your copy to succeed, and you probably want more work from the client too. So it's only natural to think about what they might prefer. The problem is that what they like personally might not be right for the project.

If you catch yourself thinking 'Ms Client/Mr Suit will like this' instead of 'this should click with the reader', that's a danger sign. Refocus on the reader and what *they* need to hear. Instead of trying to impress the client with the copy itself, impress them with the thinking behind it. For example, you could add comments to your copy explaining your thinking, or write a separate commentary outlining your strategy. Even if you don't show it to the client, it might help you justify your decisions later on.

Answer the reader back

If you know how the reader might respond to what you're saying, you can even answer them back. For example, here's a drink ad that uses this technique to play on the unfamiliarity of the product:

> Kopparberg fruit lager.
> Yeah, lager.

By doing this throughout longer copy, you can build up one side of the conversation with your reader, so you respond to their questions and objections as they come up. Obviously, you can't be sure *exactly* what they'll be thinking. But you can make an educated guess by challenging the last thing you've written with questions like 'so what?' (as we saw in chapter 3). Here's an example:

Copy	Reader's thoughts
Weighs fewer pounds. Costs fewer too. [Picture of laptop]	Ha, nice gag. I've been thinking about getting a laptop, so I'll read a bit more.
The *TopLap 3000* is the thinnest laptop you can buy.	So what?
It's as small and light as a magazine, so you really can take it anywhere.	OK, but is it any good?
Its *Octium III* processor and 8GB of RAM mean plenty of power for work or games, and the battery keeps going for up to ten hours.	High spec. Sounds expensive.
And with prices from just £499, it's never been easier to get a *TopLap* in your life.	Get real. I'm not buying it without trying it out.
Drop into *Laptops-R-Us* any time to see it for yourself.	I might just do that...

As the example shows, this technique can help to give your copy structure and flow. You start with where the reader is now, decide where you want them to end up, and use their anticipated responses to write the steps in between.

Use 'we' (or even 'I')

If the reader is 'you', the company or brand that is talking should be 'we'. That works more naturally for some brands and projects than for others, but it should always be the first thing you try. Otherwise you end up talking about yourself in the third person, like *Flex Gym* do in the first example above, which is confusing. People rarely talk about themselves this way in conversation, and it sounds pretty weird if they do. So brands shouldn't do it in copy either.

One step on from that is the product itself speaking to the reader, as in this example from the back of a National Express coach:

I'm always cheaper if you book in advance

It's certainly punchy. If you didn't use 'I', you'd have to say 'this coach' or 'travelling on this coach', which is weaker, or rephrase the line completely. It's also memorable, and strikes up a relationship between the passenger and the coach before a ticket is even bought.

Here's another talking vehicle – this time, a Salvation Army van:

Fill me with hope.

For every full bag you donate, you help us give hope to those who need it most. Thank you!

The play on words, and humanising the van as one of the team, makes the message much more engaging. But some might say that making objects talk like this is just a bit twee. I guess it's just a matter of taste.

Write like you talk

If copy is a conversation, it should sound like someone talking. But sometimes people write in a certain style because they feel that's how writing *should* sound. They know what they want to say, and could easily tell you if you asked them. But when they sit down at a keyboard, it comes out 'writerly' – too formal, too flowery or too fussy. Things get even worse when they need to ask readers to do something, because it's easy to mistake formality for authority.

Here's an example that I saw in a local café:

NOTICE

We would kindly request that customers refrain from disposing of nappies and sanitary towels down the toilet and ask that you make use of the disposal bins provided

Thank you

What they really meant to say was:

No nappies or sanitary towels down the toilet please

Please don't put rubbish down the toilet. Use the bin instead.

Thanks.

Ironically, writerly writing can sometimes be quicker to do. Maybe that's because it often talks about the writer's own concerns, and thinking about our own problems comes easily, whereas concentrating on the reader takes more effort. Or maybe it's because we're used to seeing that stuff in print, so we reach for it as a way to fill a blank page. Whatever the reason, if your first draft does end up a bit writerly, you'll probably want to go back and make it more conversational later on. As novelist Elmore Leonard put it, 'If it sounds like writing, I rewrite it.'

Writing like you talk generally means using shorter, simpler words and sentences. It's OK to use contractions like 'it's' and 'we're', and phrases that aren't full sentences. Basically, if you read your copy out loud, it should feel natural and flowing, like something you could actually say. If you trip over the words, or it feels like a bit of mouthful, rephrase it.

John E. Kennedy famously defined advertising as 'salesmanship in print'. If you can, chat to salespeople or support staff who actually deal with customers. They often know excellent ways to talk about products, services and benefits that have never found their way into their company's marketing or even been written down – until now. To get them talking, try a little role-play: 'Imagine I'm a prospect who's just called your office. How would you describe the service to me?'

Write for someone you know

Legendary American adman Fairfax Cone used to ask copywriters, 'Would you say that to someone you know?'

It's a great test if you think your copy might be getting a bit writerly. For each sentence, just ask yourself, 'Would I say this out loud, to a real person?' Or just say it out loud to yourself and see how it sounds. What would you think if someone said that to you? And how would you feel?

In chapter 4, we saw how developing a persona can help you understand the reader. You *could* try writing for your persona – the only problem being that the person you imagined doesn't actually exist, so it's a rather academic exercise. So how about writing for a real person you know instead? Choose a partner, parent, sibling, best friend or longstanding colleague who might buy the product, and persuade them to try it.

As we saw in chapter 1, readers aren't waiting with bated breath for your copy. They're busy getting stuff done or having fun. So for even more realism, imagine you're speaking to your real-world person in a situation that has nothing to do with the product. For example, you're playing pool or getting ready to go out with your best friend, and you've got to get them interested in insurance. What will you say?

You don't want to waste their time, so you'll keep your copy simple and to the point. You don't want to embarrass yourself, so you won't make weak jokes, or use flashy words that are hard to say out loud. You'll simply tell them what they need to know, answer their likely questions and make your case as strongly as you can. And while that might not give your copy everything it needs, it will probably be a very good start.

Use the same words the reader uses

To make your conversation with the reader flow, use the same words they use.

Matching the reader's language obviously helps them understand you. But it also shows that *you* understand *them*. It says that you like them, you respect them and you're both on the same level. It shows that you really care about the conversation, and you want it to work.

On the other hand, if you use obscure, formal or technical words, it's harder for readers to understand what you mean. It sounds like you're talking down to them and don't particularly like them. It says that you don't really care what they think, and that it's up to them to work out what you mean. And it shuts out people with less reading ability, so they can't understand your message even if they want to.

Recently, I was queuing to use an ATM when a woman turned around to ask me what this on-screen message meant:

> Please enter the amount required in multiples of £10.

Clearly, words like 'amount' 'require' and 'multiple' didn't mean that much to her. And that's hardly surprising, because the reading age of this sentence is around 12, but the average reading age in the UK is nine.[41] Around a quarter of UK adults would fail GCSE English,[42] so imagine how they would struggle – never mind non-native speakers, or people with learning difficulties, or people with dementia.

Since cashpoints are for everyone, the words they use should be clear to as many people as possible. A better version would be something like:

> Type in how much money you want. This machine only has £10 and £20 notes in it.

Yes, it's terribly clunky, with a rhythm like potatoes falling on to the floor. But it's so simple that a child could understand it: the reading age of this version is just seven.

41 www.see-a-voice.org/marketing-ad/effective-communication/readability/
42 www.literacytrust.org.uk/adult_literacy/illiterate_adults_in_england

And that's the right approach when you really need the reader to understand, but have no idea how well they read.

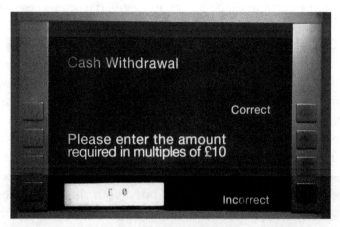

Incorrect language – or rather, using the wrong words – puts barriers in the reader's way

Sometimes, firms want to make their products sound more impressive than they really are. So instead of saying they do 'boiler repairs', they say they offer something like 'heating solutions'. But instead of impressing their customers, they're really just putting doubt in their minds: can these guys repair my boiler or not?

This is even more crucial when you think about the way we find products online. If people are searching for 'tree cutting', do you really want your site to be all about 'gardening and landscape solutions'? Search marketing offers firms a stark choice: use the words that customers type into Google, or lose website traffic to a competitor.

Fortunately, it's easy to find out what people are searching for. Google Trends (trends.google.com) lets you track the popularity of different words and phrases over time and suggests alternatives.

For example, at the time of writing, 'boiler repair' scores 67% against 29% for 'heating solutions' over the last 12 months. But 'gas boiler repair' is the top term, with 100%. That suggests that it's worthwhile including the word 'gas' in online copy about boiler repairs, even if it seems obvious that you're talking about gas boilers.

One step on from that, Answer the Public (answerthepublic.com) uses Google AutoComplete data to suggest questions, phrases and comparisons related to a keyword or phrase. That can show you the sort of language people tend to use about your product, as well as suggesting ways to answer their most frequently asked questions.

These data-driven tools make it much easier to build a case for using the reader's language. You may be convinced that a particular phrase is right, but if your client disagrees, it's just your opinion against theirs. With hard data, you've got the reader's voice on your side.

See it from the reader's side

Remember the bridge from chapter 1? You're standing on one side, and your reader's on the other. Your job is to get them to cross over. So what will you do?

You could stay where you are and yell at them about how nice it is over here. Or you could cross over, have a look around and a chat, and *then* point out a few reasons to cross.

If you did that, your reader would know you understood their situation as well as your own. And you wouldn't even have to shout.

One way to see the reader's side is to link the benefits of the product to their situation. For example:

A home office without the distractions

WorkPod is a self-contained office that goes in your garden. So if there's a lot going on at home, you've always got a quiet spot where you can hide out and work undisturbed.

That's fine as far as it goes. But what if we go right over to the other side of the bridge by starting with the reader's situation and *then* crossing over to the benefits?

How can you work if you can't even hear yourself think?

The kids are screaming. The TV's blaring. The phone's ringing. Wouldn't you love to have a quiet, comfortable office that was *at* home, but not actually *in* it?

Now the copy starts with what the reader wants to change, instead of what we want to say. That's much more likely to engage them from the start. It shows empathy and builds the foundation for persuasion. And last but by no means least, it gives us a ready-made headline and opening.

Be concrete

Check out this example of bad writing. (It's fictitious, but not unrealistic.)

Applications can be lodged via the *DBD* online portal. Since no further correspondence will be entered into, applicants are reminded to ensure that the information provided is fully accurate and complete before commencing the application process.

The main reason why this sounds stuffy and obscure is that the language is too abstract. It's all about *ideas* rather than *things*. There's too much distance between the words and the world.

Now here's the same thing using more concrete language:

You can apply at our website. We can't answer any letters or emails, so before you start, remember to

163

make sure you've told us everything we need to know, and that you haven't made any mistakes.

This version refers much more directly to real-world objects and events, with more images that readers will recognise from everyday life. For example, instead of 'correspondence', there are 'letters and emails'. Instead of 'applicants', it's 'you'. Since the reader doesn't have to decode any abstract language, they quickly get a very clear picture of what they need to do.

Sometimes, people shy away from concrete language because they feel it's not official or businesslike enough. Maybe all those images sound too much like a child's picture book. But you can pay a high price for an abstract, corporate tone, particularly when you're writing for people whose first language isn't English. When in doubt, go for concrete language every time.

Use verbs, not nouns

The second *DBD* example above also uses more verbs (doing words) and fewer nouns (naming words). The first version is full of nouns that are actually events: 'applications', 'correspondence', 'information' and 'application process'. In the second version, they've been turned into verbs: 'apply', 'answer', 'tell' and 'start'. That makes the writing simpler, clearer and shorter.

Verbs are more concrete because they say what is actually going on, rather than giving it a label. For example, if I ask you to imagine eating an apple, or walking through a forest, it's easy for you to picture those things. In fact, you'll probably find it hard *not* to picture them. But what if I ask you to visualise the consumption of fresh fruit, or reflect on perambulation through an arboreal environment? The ideas are the same, but it's far less obvious what I'm talking about, and you probably don't get such a clear picture in your head.

People sometimes use noun phrases as a defence mechanism, because they don't want to talk about what's really happening, or who it's happening to. Or they may go straight to the language of their own working lives – where they deal with 'applications', 'correspondence' and 'applicants', for example. But as we've seen, copy needs to 'face outwards' towards the reader, not inwards towards the writer's concerns.

Be active

Normally, the subject of a sentence is whoever or whatever is doing something, while the object is what they do it to. In the sentence 'I opened the door', the subject is 'I', the object is 'the door' and the verb is 'opened'.

The passive voice is when the subject of a sentence is acted on by the verb, so it's not clear who's doing what. For example, if I say 'The door was opened' you know what happened (opening), and what it happened to (the door), but not who did it.

The first example above uses the passive voice three times, while the second one switches to the active equivalents:

Passive voice	Active equivalent
Applications can be lodged	You can apply
No correspondence will be entered into	We can't answer
Applicants are reminded	Remember

With the active voice, we can clearly see who will do what. The reader ('you') needs to apply and remember things, while the organisation ('we') won't answer letters.

It's nearly always better to use the active voice, but the passive has its place. It's useful when you want to talk about an event without saying directly who's responsible for it. For example, instead of yelling, 'You left the oven on again!' I could gently observe, 'The oven's been left on again.' This might be useful if you needed to write a letter to a customer tactfully pointing out that they'd made a mistake, or forgotten to do something (for example, 'Your account has not yet been activated').

Be specific

When you're aiming to impress the reader, it's easy to reach for impressive-sounding words like 'powerful', 'innovative', 'comprehensive' and so on. But they bring the same problems as abstract language: too much distance between words and reality. Those claims may sound big, but unfortunately they're also pretty hollow. You need to give readers some proof, so they can clearly see what you're promising and how it's different from the competition.

An easy way to drill down to specifics is to ask 'How?' For whatever big word you want to use, just ask *'How* is it...?' That will often bring you to something more specific that will work much better in your copy.

Here are some examples:

Non-specific claim	Ask...	Specific claim
Our find-a-freelance service is truly innovative.	How is it innovative?	It's the first one where you can talk directly to the person handling your project, in real time.
We provide excellent customer service.	How it is excellent?	We reply to every customer email within 24 hours.
Loobrite is a highly effective toilet cleaner.	How is it effective?	It kills 99.9% of germs.
We've created a powerful new online platform for managing multiple projects.	How is it powerful?	You can manage up to 20 projects at once, each with a team of 10 members.

If you're talking about things that can be counted, you can be specific by giving exact numbers. That projects confidence, because it shows you don't need rhetorical tricks to big yourself up. The numbers speak for themselves, as in this online copy from Unbound, the crowdfunded publishing platform:

> Over 134,079 people from every corner of the globe have supported an Unbound project and helped make that idea a reality. To date, we've published 280 books that only exist thanks to the Unbound community.

If you use numbers, they need to sound good – whatever 'good' means in context. If Unbound had only published nine books, that wouldn't sound so great. On the other hand, if they'd published thousands, authors might worry that the bar was set too low. The figure of 280 suggests both solid experience and a commitment to quality.

Specifics are details. So you might assume they belong deep inside your copy, not in the headline or opening. But if they express an important benefit, they can work just as well upfront. That's what journalists mean when they say 'don't bury the lead'.

This copy from London Metropolitan University targets potential students by speaking to one of their main concerns:

Employers love us

95% of our graduates are in work or further study within six months

This is from an online ad (see image overleaf). So when readers see it, they're probably thinking about something else, and may know nothing at all about the university. But if they're choosing a college, and have given even the slightest thought to their future prospects, the promise of a near-certain career path is bound to draw them in.

Leading with a strong specific claim to get readers' attention.
REPRODUCED BY KIND PERMISSION OF LONDON METROPOLITAN UNIVERSITY

Make it real

In chapter 3, we saw that what really sells a product is the experience of using it, not the product itself – the sizzle, not the sausage. Your copy can bring that experience to life and make the reader want it.

Literary critic Viktor Shklovsky said, 'Art exists that one may recover the sensation of life; it exists to make one feel things, to make the stone stony.'[43] He suggested that the most powerful art used 'defamiliarisation' to make everyday things new and interesting again, so people could see them in a new light. Copywriting can do something similar with sensory language: describing the sights, sounds, smells, tastes and textures of using a product.

Sensory experiences key directly into our memories, and those memories often trigger strong emotions. So sensory language can evoke the *feeling* of using a product, as well as the physical experience of it.

Marketers sometimes talk about 'moments of truth'. The first moment of truth is when people encounter the product for the first time, and decide whether to buy it. The second

43 'Art as Technique' in *Theory of Prose* by Viktor Shklovsky, Dalkey Archive Press, 1993.

is when they actually use it, and form their opinion of it. The third is when they decide whether to buy it again, or recommend it to others.

Sensory language mentally transports the reader from the first moment of truth to the second. Instead of just reading facts about a product or being told about its benefits, they're 'pre-experiencing' it in their minds and imagining how it will fit into their life.

Crucially, they're also pre-experiencing having *already decided to buy it*. For as long as they stay in that future moment, their purchase is a done deal. That helps them get used to the idea of buying for real.

A very sensual example of this is food writing, like the descriptions on a restaurant menu. They're often rich in details of tastes and textures, to help you mentally sample each dish. By the time you decide what you're going to have, your brain's eaten the entire menu.

Potato skins

Crispy baked skins stuffed with juicy stir-fried mushrooms and white wine or succulent minced lamb with pine nuts

That's the obvious way to make food sound appealing. But there's always a sensual side to a product experience, if you want to bring it out. Here's the copy of a 2016 TV ad used by David Lloyd Clubs, a UK chain of sports and health clubs:[44]

Put your phone in the locker. Your keys in the locker. Work, that traffic jam – put *everything* in the locker. Don't dilly. Don't dally. You have a heart: use it. You have senses: switch them on. In a place where you're

44 Watch it at tinyurl.com/davidlloydclubs

more than just a number. And when you flop on the sofa at the end of the day, you'll know that was a day well spent.

The voiceover was accompanied by imagery of people really getting into their workouts, making something that people might think of as a chore look like an absolute joy. On the emotional side, the image of putting 'everything' in the locker is an elegant metaphor for forgetting about everyday worries and pressures (see 'Find a metaphor' in chapter 9).

Here's another great example from First Direct, the online bank:

Future you is enjoying the new car smell

The product, car finance, is pretty dull. But by focusing on the enjoyment of a smell, this copy turns something dry and boring into a promise of pleasure. The mindbending 'future you' idea explicitly transports the reader forward in time, past buying and paying, to the sensual payoff of sitting in their new car for the very first time.

Sometimes, the experience might be one the reader has never had before. So you need to reassure them that it's going to be fun, safe, easy or just not scary. The soft drink Dr Pepper®, which has always had niche appeal, played on this with its slogan:

What's the worst that could happen?

Or it might be something that's become old and familiar that you want the reader to rediscover or re-evaluate, like the experience of eating Kellogg's Corn Flakes®:

Have you forgotten how good they taste?

It might even be a bad experience that the product can prevent, or at least make better. Here's another example from First Direct:

Burst pipe in the middle of the night insurance

This transports the reader forward to something they definitely *don't* want to experience. But if they have to go through it, they know that any help would be much appreciated.

There's no reason why B2B copy can't use sensory language. But B2B services tend to be more spread out over time or space, which makes it harder to boil them down to a single vivid experience. So sometimes it's better to prepare the reader for the whole process of buying and using them.

Athletes prepare for a race by picturing themselves winning it. Once we've experienced something, even if it's only in our imagination, it becomes more familiar. Then, when we live through it for real, it feels less threatening, because we've 'been there before'.

Here's some copy that encourages the reader to pre-experience a B2B service:

> From the very first time you call us, you'll appreciate the way we listen to what you really need and shape our service around it. Our support team will be on site throughout the setup process to help your team members learn all about our software. And once you're up and running, you can get in touch any time by phone or email for unlimited customer support.

There isn't much sensory description, but the idea is the same. As the reader reads through this story, they can 'see' the steps they'll follow and imagine what each one will be like. Now, making an enquiry is less of a leap in the dark. On the emotional side, words like 'appreciate', 'listen', 'need' and 'help' reassure them that this will be a relationship between people, not just a transaction between firms.

Stay positive

It's hard for your mind to focus on a negative. If I say 'don't think of an elephant', you immediately picture an elephant. That's because you can't help picking up on the image in the sentence, even though the other words are telling you not to. Concrete language is so powerful that it bursts out of its grammatical box.

These mental processes can have a big impact on personal decisions. For example, many smokers want to give up, for health or money reasons. But because they frame their goal as 'stop smoking', their minds stay focused on the very thing they want to avoid. 'Anywhere but here' is not a useful destination. Once smokers shift their attention to saving money, getting healthier and becoming more attractive, they find it easier to begin their journey.

Because of this, you'll usually want to frame your language positively rather than negatively. That means talking about what you *do* want people to do, think or feel – not what you don't. Here are some examples:

Instead of...	...write
Lose weight	Get slim
Reduce waste	Make better use of resources
Reduce your workload	Enjoy more free time
We don't do things by halves	We're with you all the way
Don't wait	Act now
Slash costs	Save money
Cut through complexity	Simplify

What about two negatives? Do they cancel each other out and make a positive? Not necessarily. Here's an envelope headline from Majestic Wine:

Four ways to never pay for wines you don't love

The double negative ('never pay' + 'don't love') turns this into a sort of mathematical formula that the reader must solve. Not paying for things is always appealing, which is probably why the line was framed this way. But the word 'pay' inevitably suggests parting with cash, even when it's negated. So maybe something like this would have been better:

Four ways to only pay for wines you love

Having said all that, there may be times when you *do* want to emphasise the negative. As we saw in chapter 7, if the product solves a problem, you might want to spend some time 'poking the problem' before offering to solve it. Here's some text from a Lakeland catalogue, for a soup-making machine, that does just that:

Soup in one simple step
No pan, no hob, no hassle

This has the ideal balance between a big, tangible, positive benefit in the headline (convenience), which is then strengthened by listing the inconvenient negative things that the product gets rid of. It would be hard to reframe that part positively, because the pan and the hob don't really have positive counterparts – in the brave new world of the soup machine, they simply disappear.

Avoid jargon and clichés (mostly)

Based on this chapter so far, you'd hardly expect me to urge you to use jargon and clichés. After all, stuffy business-speak and worn-out phrases could never engage the reader, right?

Actually, it depends.

Let's take jargon first. Sometimes, it's a writerly attempt to bamboozle the reader with obscure language, or impress them with trendy buzzwords. Obviously, that doesn't make for engaging copy.

However, not all jargon is the same. Sometimes, it's actually domain language: the specialised words and phrases used by a certain group of people. If you use it yourself, you might engage those people while excluding others – and that might be exactly what you want. This online ad for hosting provider TransIP takes this approach to the extreme:

Blade VPS. Pure SSD

```
<ul>
<li> 99.99% uptime </li>
<li> KVM </li>
<li> 100 Gb/s network </li>
</ul>
```

What does it all mean? I've no idea. But that doesn't matter, because the ad isn't aimed at me. The defiantly opaque acronyms and HTML tags make it very clear that this is an ad for internet geeks. (Incidentally, this is also an example of features that don't need to be turned into benefits, because the target reader will happily do that for themselves.)

TransIP uses geek-speak to attract and entertain its target readers.
REPRODUCED BY KIND PERMISSION OF TRANSIP

Other possibilities might include using emojis for younger readers, literary allusions for bookworms or specialised language for hobbyists and enthusiasts. With copy like this, the medium is the message. You're *showing* the reader that you understand them, not just telling them. You are, quite literally, speaking their language.

However, domain language comes with a health warning: you must get it right. If you use niche terms even slightly out of place, your reader will instantly see that you don't know what you're talking about, leaving you worse off than before. Avoid the trap by asking your knowledgeable client to check your copy with this in mind.

So what about clichés? Should you really avoid them like the plague?

Clichés are phrases – often metaphors – that have lost their impact through overuse. In his famous essay 'Politics and the English Language', George Orwell told journalists never to use 'a metaphor, simile, or other figure of speech which you are used to seeing in print'.[45] He knew that familiarity breeds contempt, and that if people don't think about the words they read, they probably won't think about the ideas behind them either. Fresh thinking demands fresh words.

Orwell wrote his rules in 1946. But if you open a newspaper today, it seems journos haven't got the memo. You'll still see stock phrases like 'political heavyweights', 'tributes pouring in', 'unsung heroes', 'landslide victories' and many more. Why?

The answer is that while some well-known phrases really are worn out and useless, others are still rich in meaning and therefore useful. There are five reasons you might want to use them.

First, they can be the hallmark of a certain voice. If a mainstream journalist referred to a senior minister as a

45   Included in *George Orwell: Essays*, Penguin Classics, 2000.

'quarterback of the political scene' or a 'Westminster sumo', we might assume they were a novice writer, or perhaps a non-native English speaker. Those alternative metaphors might be fresher, but they just don't sound right. Handling the tools of the trade competently gives you authority – and words are some of the most important tools there are. (We'll come back to authority in chapter 13, and tone of voice in chapter 15.)

Second, clichés are shortcuts. The whole reason they become popular in the first place is because they express a particular idea very well. Yes, writers may resort to them because they can't be bothered to think of something new. But readers are lazy too – or, at least, they're miserly with their cognitive energy. Sometimes, a cliché is simply the quickest and most direct route to the destination.

Third, well-known sayings can be persuasive, because they express things that 'everybody' knows to be true. They can remind us of stories that contain instructive morals or psychological truths, but in an incredibly concise way – as in the expressions 'sour grapes' or 'cry wolf'.[46] By using these phrases, you give your argument a grounding in our shared culture. When you summon up folk wisdom that readers agree with, they're more likely to accept the other things you say.[47] (This is a kind of social proof, which we'll see in chapter 13.)

For example, if you were writing about anti-virus software, you could capture an important benefit with 'prevention is better than cure'. Or you could tempt the reader to snarf down a sticky cake by saying 'a little of what you fancy does you good'. You wouldn't gain much by rewriting these phrases – or, at least, the originality you gained might be less than the persuasiveness you lost.

46 See 'The Fox and the Grapes' and 'The Boy Who Cried Wolf' in any edition of Aesop's Fables.
47 To learn more about the stories, myths and meanings behind familiar phrases, see *Brewer's Dictionary of Phrase and Fable* by Dr Ebenezer Cobham Brewer, Chambers, 2013.

Fourth, established phrases can be more vivid and concrete than the alternative. If you're writing for a B2B reader, 'bread-and-butter work' is more vivid than something like 'day-to-day projects'. In a context where it's easy to get lost in abstraction, anything you can touch or see goes a long way.

Finally, clichés are, by definition, familiar, and that puts the reader at their ease. Familiar things are easier for us to understand, so we feel that they're safer or more reliable, or that whatever they describe will also be easy to do. Psychologists call this 'cognitive fluency'.[48] So if you want to strike a comforting or reassuring tone, you probably don't want to use too much adventurous language.

For example, here's a classic slogan for Dairylea cheese spread (Mondelēz International):

> Kids will eat it till the cows come home.

Using such a timeworn phrase does make this line a bit, er, cheesy. But if the reader is a tired parent with limited mental bandwidth, a stock phrase might appeal more than something radical – like this excellent but bizarre slogan for Chedds (Dairy Crest):

> Chedds be Cheddar. Cheddar be Chedds.

Let's be clear. I'm not suggesting that you deliberately stuff your copy with the weakest, most predictable clichés you can think of. All I'm saying is that you might *choose* to use familiar phrases in certain situations. If a cliché really is the best way to reach your reader, use it.

Tell a story

Storytelling is one of the copywriter's most powerful tools. It's hot right now, but marketers were using it for decades before brands had 'chief storytelling officers'. And that's

48 'If it's easy to read, it's easy to do, pretty, good, and true' by Hyunjin Song and Norbert Schwarz, *The Psychologist*, vol. 23, February 2010, pp. 108–111.

not surprising, because stories have so many things going for them.

Stories are how we make sense of the world. We hear them as soon as we can talk, so they tap into our deepest memories and emotions. When we read them as children, they show us how things work, and prepare us for things we've yet to experience. As adults, we use them to talk about our memories, our problems and our emotions, and to describe our relationships with each other. Stories aren't just like life; they *are* life.

Stories can do magic. They take us away to other places that are completely removed from our experience, yet perfectly familiar. Cognitive psychologist Keith Oatley has found that when we read a story, 'we create our own version of the piece of fiction, our own dream, our own enactment'.[49] In the process, we use the same parts of our brains as if we were really watching or living through the events of the story, drawing on our own past experience to reconstruct it in our heads.

Stories are powerful. Once we're drawn in, we have to go with the flow. We surrender to the will of the storyteller and accept their way of seeing the world, at least for a while. And if we want to know how things turn out, we have to stay with the story until the end.

All this means that stories are much more than just another writing technique. When we read them, we have a completely different experience from when we merely digest information or compare benefits. Stories are unique.

Stories can help your copywriting in many ways. They're memorable, so they're a good way to tell people things you want them to remember. They feature people, events and emotions from real life, which adds human interest to a message that might otherwise be a bit dry. And because

49 *Such Stuff as Dreams: The Psychology of Fiction* by Keith Oatley, Wiley, 2011.

we're mentally 'hard-wired' to pay attention to stories and remember their lessons, they can be very persuasive.

If you're writing about a customer's experience, your copy can naturally take the shape of a story. Here's a simple example from Weldfix:

Welding a Metal Gate Hinge

This gate hinge had rusted and broken. We made a welding repair to the gate hinge and now it works again. If you have a London gate in need of repair, give us a call.

It's ultra-basic, but it still has the three essential elements of a case study: problem, action and solution. This form is the same as the 'hero's journey' that drives many of the most famous myths, novels, plays and films. The hero or heroine hears the call to adventure, overcomes a challenge and returns home transformed into someone new. You can use the same formula with almost any product or service, to tell the story of how it solves a problem or makes a change, or how the customer uses it.

If you're writing about a company, you could write its history as a story. Or you could tell the story of how a product was created or developed. Here's a story I wrote for Heat Holders®, the UK thermal clothing brand, for its product packaging:

The Heat Holders story

Back in 2006, Heat Holders inventor David Doughty was watching his son play rugby when he realised his feet were freezing, even though he was wearing so-called 'thermal' socks. At that moment, he decided he would create a new kind of thermal sock. One so blissfully warm that his feet wouldn't know it was winter.

Case study, customer journey, problem/solution

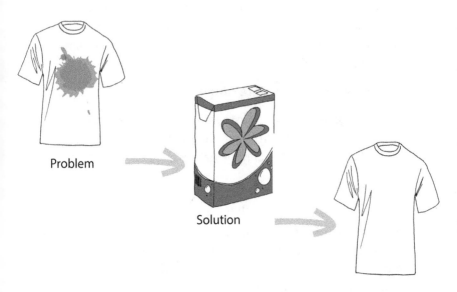

Hero's journey

Case studies (and other marketing stories) can take the same basic
structure as the hero's journey

After two years of hard work, the unique Heat Holders socks appeared in stores. People absolutely loved them, and they were deservedly granted a UK patent. Since then, we've also added hats, gloves, leggings and more to the range, all with the same philosophy: it's all about the warmth.

This has several features that might work for your copy too. First, it's mostly about people, events and emotions, rather than companies, products and features. Second, it's relatable, because it describes the familiar experience of having cold feet and the satisfaction of finding a product that actually works. Finally, it's not too self-absorbed: there's only one 'we', and the rest is about inventor David and the people who now enjoy his product.

Interesting stories have some ups and downs. There's some drama or conflict along the way to a happy ending, just as the hero has to overcome a challenge before returning home. That challenge can take many forms: rivals or enemies (whether human or corporate), circumstances and events, or even forces of nature. Or the hero might just struggle with themselves, trying to become better or more powerful somehow. In the Heat Holders story, the challenge is David's terrible socks, which he overcomes by inventing something better.

Here's part of the company story presented by Innocent Drinks on its website:[50]

The fairly boring bit

They [the three founders] write a business plan. Nobody wants to invest (to be fair, it did look a bit boring, see left). They re-write the plan another 11 times. Every bank, venture capitalist and business angel in London turns them down.

---

50 You can read the whole thing at innocentdrinks.co.uk/us/our-story

Thank you Mr Pinto

> A desperate email is sent to everyone they know, with the subject "Does anyone know anyone rich?" Enter a nice man called Mr Pinto, without whom…

Many firms wouldn't want to dwell on a failure to attract investors – even if they got funding in the end – because it might suggest their business plans were weak. By admitting that they faced a challenge, Innocent give their story more honesty and emotion, so it doesn't end up as corporate self-congratulation. Ironically, what they call the 'fairly boring bit' actually adds interest.[51]

Some briefs might call for a story that includes more challenge – or is *all* challenge. Here's an ad for an alcohol abuse charity that simply presents the harrowing story of one of its clients, in their own words:

> Hi, my name is Saule. I am fifty-two years old now. I started drinking beer when I was fourteen. Over time, I got hooked on hard liquor, drinking more than one liter a day. My family left me as it was impossible for them to live with me. I am now alone and at high risk of getting cirrhosis. I don't want to lose my life as well. I need help.

Here, the reader themselves must provide the happy ending, by supporting the charity. The problem is Saule's plight, and the solution is the reader's response.

Finally, a word of caution. Stories are great, but they're not a magic bullet. Your copy won't automatically interest people just because you say it's a story, particularly if it's short on human characters or drama. What's more, even a strong story won't necessarily attract the same commitment that your reader gives to the novel they're reading, or even

51 For more on what makes a good story, see my blog post at abccopywriting.com/goodstory

their Facebook feed. You're telling your story on a street corner, not at bedtime, and your audience can walk away any time they like. Respect their attention by giving them a story you'd want to read yourself.

Once upon a time

Think of a story you could tell about your own life. What challenge have you taken on and overcome? How would you make it interesting to a reader?

12

SHARPEN UP YOUR COPY

Revise your copy to make it as good as you can.

Rewrite, rewrite, rewrite

I won't bore you with the story of how I wrote this book. But let's just say I wouldn't want you to read my first draft. In fact, I'd guess that I spent three times as long editing as I did writing, if not more.

While creative ideas can come in a flash, most copywriters need some revision to reach a version they're happy with. Often, most of the craft of writing, and a lot of what you might call 'inspiration', actually happens *after* the first draft is done. That's what Ernest Hemingway meant when he said, 'All writing is rewriting.'

Here are a few points to consider as you rewrite, some of which are covered in more detail in the rest of this chapter:

Length	Is your copy too long, or too short?
	Have you said everything you need to say, no more and no less?
	Have you said enough to get the reader from where they are to where you want them to be?

Focus	Is there a single clear theme, or (for longer copy) a clear theme for each section or paragraph?
	Does the body copy deliver on the promise of the headline? For longer copy, does each section deliver on the promise of its subheading?
	Are there places where you're trying to do two things at once? If so, would it be better to do them separately, or do just one of them?
	Are there any weaker parts that you could cut out and make what's left even stronger?
	Have you wandered away from the main argument? If so, should you move those bits somewhere else, or just delete them?
Duplication	Does each part add something unique in terms of benefits, persuasion, information, feeling or tone?
	Have you made the same point twice anywhere? One version is always better, so choose that and delete the other.
	Have you used the same word or phrase twice anywhere? Vary the wording unless there's a good reason not to (such as using domain language, optimising for SEO, etc).
Order	Do the ideas follow on from each other in a logical way? Are there any missing links or wrong steps in your argument?
	Do you talk about the main benefit first, and sub-benefits later on?
	If one point depends on another point being made first, do they appear in the right order?
Pace	Does your copy unfold at a consistent pace?
	Is the pace right for the mood of the copy? Are any parts too hurried, or too slow?
	If the pace varies, is there a good reason for this? And does the effect work?

Paragraphs	Does each paragraph deal with a particular idea?
	Do the paragraph breaks fall at logical points?
	Are the paragraphs the right length for the reading medium (print, digital, mobile and so on)?
	Do paragraph lengths vary?
Sentences	Do most of your sentences have a nice, simple structure – like 'subject, verb, object'?
	Have you used the passive voice (see 'Be active' in chapter 11)? If so, do you want to?
	Would any sentences be simpler if they were split, or if the parts were in a different order?
	Are any sentences too long? (You should be able to say each one in a single breath.)
	Have you got a good mix of shorter and longer sentences?
Phrases	Are there any phrases that could be replaced by single words?
	Have you used any obscure language or clichés? Are you sure you want to? (See 'Avoid jargon and clichés (mostly)' in chapter 11.)
Individual words	Is this the right word for what you want to say?
	Is there a simpler or more commonly used word with the same meaning? Would that be better?
	Have you used an abstract noun where it would be better to use a concrete verb? (For example, 'excavation' instead of 'digging a hole'.)
	Do you need to explain what any words mean (acronyms, scientific terms, specialised terms and so on)? Or would it be better to just avoid them completely?
Description	Does all your description serve a purpose?
	Are all your adjectives and adverbs worth including? Would anything be better described with verbs?
	Have you described anything that will be obvious in other ways – for example, from a photo?

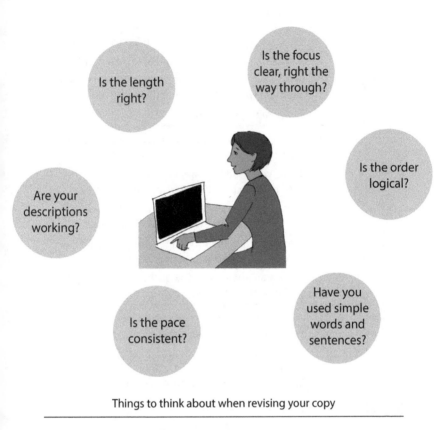

Things to think about when revising your copy

Make it simple

With copy, simpler is nearly always better – for these six simple reasons.

- **Simple words are primary**. They're the first ones we learn, so they're the most familiar to us. They're the building blocks of what we know. But they're not like toys, because we never outgrow them. They stay with us for life.
- **Simple words are strong**. They're solid and reliable. You can be sure of them. As Dave Trott says, 'All the strength is in simplicity, and all the weakness is in complexity.'[52]

---

52 See his keynote at the 2013 Copywriting Conference: tinyurl.com/davetrott

- **Simple words are honest**. As Euripides said, 'The language of truth is simple.' When your writing has the ring of truth, it's much easier to build trust and persuade the reader. Simple words *feel* true because we use them for life's biggest, most important messages – things like 'I love you', 'It's a girl' or 'I got the job'.
- **Simple words are clear**. They have one meaning that everyone knows. Putting your ideas into simple words forces you to get them clear in your mind. What's more, researchers have found that readers see people who write simply as *more* intelligent, not less.[53]
- **Simple words are easy.** The simpler your words, the easier and quicker it is for people to understand them. So using simple words shows respect for the reader. By writing simply, you're saying, 'I know you're busy, and you didn't ask for this message. So I've done my best to make it easy to read, to save you time and effort.'
- **Simple words are inclusive.** The simpler your words, the more people can understand you. Simple words are accessible to the widest possible audience. As content expert Sarah Richards says, 'It's not dumbing down. It's opening up.'[54] You could even argue that writing simply is a moral duty – a sort of verbal democracy.

For all these reasons, if you write simply, the reader is more likely to understand, remember and act on your words. And as a copywriter, that's exactly what you want.[55]

However, copy that's simple to read isn't always easy to write. Making copy simple takes so much concentration that the effort can feel almost physical, like lifting heavy bricks into place.

---

53 'Consequences of erudite vernacular utilized irrespective of necessity: problems with using long words needlessly' by Daniel M. Oppenheimer, *Applied Cognitive Psychology*, vol. 20(2).

54 *Content Design* by Sarah Richards, Content Design London, 2017, p. 37.

55 For more advice on writing simply, see *Plain Words* by Ernest Gowers and Rebecca Gowers, Penguin, 2015, and *The Elements of Style* by William Strunk Jr. and E.B. White, Pearson, 1999 (often known as 'Strunk and White').

Simple words are...

Primary
We learn simple words first and
remember them all our lives

Strong
Simple words are solid
and reliable

Honest
Simple words have
the ring of truth

Clear
Simple words have one
meaning that everyone knows

Easy
Simple words give the reader
less work to do

Inclusive
The simpler your words,
the more people can
understand you

Six reasons why simple words are better

Of course, your reader will never know all this. If no one notices your work, you've done it well. As Nathaniel Hawthorne said, 'Easy reading is damn hard writing.'

You might expect the first thing you write to be the simplest, but in fact it's usually the other way round. Most of your first drafts will be too long and messy. You'll throw in words and phrases without really thinking, or let your ideas tumble out in random order, or wander off the point. As you rewrite, your job is to find the simple words behind the complex ones.

Simple writing flows from clear thinking and deep knowledge. Albert Einstein said, 'If you can't explain it simply, you don't understand it well enough.' For the copywriter, that means knowing enough about the product, the benefits and the reader to know what to put in and what to leave out. It's not enough just to say fewer things; they've got to be the *right* things too.

A simple rule for simplicity is *say one thing*. Introduce one big theme, or one key benefit, with your headline. If you use sections, cover one subject in each one, and state it clearly in the heading. Make each paragraph develop one idea, and introduce that idea in the first sentence. Make each sentence express one point.

The flip side of that is *don't say things twice*. Don't use two words (or two phrases, or two sentences) where one would do. Make sure every word is there for a reason.

Another useful guide is *keep the aim in mind*. Every part of your copy should move you towards the aim you identified in chapter 5. Anything that doesn't can go. If you find cutting difficult, think of it as improving what remains, rather than throwing something valuable away – like pruning a rose bush to get more flowers.

Give most of your sentences simple structures. Bob Levenson was one of the greatest copywriters ever and the creator of the immortal Volkswagen ads of the 1960s.

Bill Bernbach described Levenson's style as 'subject, verb, object', because nearly every sentence he wrote fell into this simple pattern.[56] Most of us learn this structure as children – even if we don't always use it as adults:

The cat	sat	on	the mat.
Subject	Verb		Object

Simple, short sentences are even more important online, and particularly when writing for mobile. The writers behind the UK government's gov.uk site work to a limit of 25 words per sentence.[57] Mobile screens can only display a certain number of words at a time, so it's harder for people to refer back without scrolling. They're likely to be distracted or inattentive as they read, and they may be in a hurry to get something done, or find something out. A useful rule of thumb is that if your sentence has more than one punctuation mark in it, it's probably too long to work on mobile.

When it comes down to individual words, simple means short, concrete and familiar. Choose words that have just one meaning, not ambiguous ones, or those that depend on context for their meaning. This helps everyone, but particularly non-native English speakers. If you do use non-standard or poetic language, you want to be sure that the risk of being less clear is worth the payoff of (possibly) being more interesting.

To give you some feedback on how simple your writing is, Microsoft Word can calculate readability statistics when it checks spelling and grammar. They'll tell you how long your words and sentences are, on average, as well as more sophisticated measures like Flesch Reading Ease and Flesch-Kincaid Grade Level. Reading Ease is a score out of 100, from

---

56 *Ugly Is Only Skin-Deep: The Story of the Ads that Changed the World* by Dominik Imseng, Matador, 2016, p. 58.
57 See the blog post at tinyurl.com/govuk25

very easy (90–100) down to college-graduate level (0–30). Plain English scores 60–70, so aim for that as a minimum. Grade level reflects how many years' education a reader would need to understand the writing; to work out the reading age, add 5. The lower your copy's reading age, the better – but it might creep up unavoidably when you're writing about certain subjects, or in a certain style.[58]

Can copy ever be *too* simple? Yes, definitely. Even though you should favour simple words and structures, you still need some variety, or your copy will sound dull and repetitive. And there will be times when the brief, or the brand's tone of voice, demands something subtle, vague or even complex. But simplicity is always a good place to start, because it shows you whether your main ideas are working. There's no point in choosing curtains if the foundations aren't sound.

Kill your darlings

This slightly alarming phrase is a warning against falling in love with your own ideas. Sometimes, you come up with something that you feel is so good, it just has to go into your copy. Soon, you're editing around it, or telling yourself why it should stay, even though you know deep down that it's not really right for the brief. You need to 'kill your darling'.

Always remember that you're the copy*writer*, not the copy*reader*. You're an actor, not the audience. Your job is to answer the brief, not please yourself. If any part of your copy isn't pulling its weight to bring reader and benefits together, it's got to go. Later on, you may also have to remind your client that your copy is aimed at their customers, not at them (see chapter 16, on responding to feedback).

The longer you work on something alone, the easier it is to lose perspective. Show your copy to a trusted friend or

58 This book has a reading ease score of 68 and a reading age of 12.4.

colleague and they'll usually put their finger on your 'darlings' straight away. Don't ignore their advice – remember, they're coming to your copy fresh, just as a reader would.

If you've had to kill some darlings to arrive at the right answer, it can seem too simple, too obvious. You think, 'Is that it?' But seeing the obvious first is what geniuses do. If your copy feels like the most natural answer to the brief, and nothing more, that's a very good sign that it's right, and will work.

This doesn't mean you shouldn't aim for creativity. If your creative idea serves the brief, you should keep it – and fight for it, if need be. But there are also times when you just need to get out of your own way, and let your copy be the way it wants to be. As Confucius said, 'You turn the handle the way it goes, not the way it ought to go.'

Stay grounded

A danger when you're writing about intangible benefits is 'laddering up'. You start at ground level with tangible benefits, then bring in intangible ones, then keep stepping up the emotional side until you end up with a generic feelgood message that has little or nothing to do with the product.

You might even climb all the way to societal benefits, where you're saying why the product improves the world. The problem is that *all* products improve the world in one small way or another. So you're not really giving readers a good reason to buy *this* product, or choose *this* firm.[59]

For example, check out this slogan for Speedo®:

> You're only one swim away from a good mood.

This copy is very strong. It's snappy, memorable, direct and grounded in real-world experience. But it's really about

---

59 'Ladder to Nowhere' by Dave Trott, *Campaign*, 10 August 2017.

swimming, not swimwear. A swim might well improve the reader's mood, but that will happen whether they're wearing the brand or not. So the message they take away might be 'Yes, I must go swimming' rather than 'Yes, I must buy Speedo®'.

Easy on the description, extra verbs

Adjectives are words that describe nouns (things), while adverbs describe verbs (actions or events). In the sentence 'The red car quickly drove off', 'red' is an adjective and 'quickly' is an adverb. Adjectives and adverbs both modify other words – in this case, 'car' and 'drove'.

You might expect these descriptive words to feature a lot in your copy. After all, don't you want to tell the reader about the product, and make the experience of using it more real? Well, yes. But some ways of doing that are better than others.

Some of the adjectives and adverbs in your first draft will be placeholders for better words you've yet to find. They're a signal that you were trying to add something to another word, to make it bigger or stronger somehow. For example:

Our training is a great way to increase your sales.

The adjective 'great' doesn't add much. It's just another way to say 'very good'. But if we roll it up with 'increase' and turn the whole lot into a concrete verb, the effect is simpler, stronger and more vivid:

Our training will skyrocket your sales.

Adverbs can weaken verbs in the same way. For example:

Stainaway quickly gets rid of tough stains.

Our main point is that *Stainaway* gets rid of tough stains. But the adverb 'quickly' is wriggling into our sentence, disrupting our 'subject, verb, object' structure and spoiling the picture we want to paint for the reader. But at the same time, speed is a benefit that we want the reader to know about. We just need a way to tell them without resorting to adverbs:

Stainaway gets rid of tough stains in a snap.

(The adjective 'tough' can stay because it's fairly concrete and adds important meaning – plus there's no one-word alternative to 'tough stains'. If we want to remind the reader about stains they've struggled to remove in the past, this is probably the best way to do it.)

Sometimes, you can replace an adverb / verb combination with a single verb that means the same thing:

A new kitchen can completely change the atmosphere of your home and substantially increase its value.

'Completely' and 'substantially' are just strengthening 'change' and 'increase'. We can swap both for single verbs:

A new kitchen can transform the atmosphere of your home and boost its value.

A potential pitfall here is changing the verb but still hanging on to the adverb, so you end up with a tautology like 'completely transform'. 'Transform' already means 'completely change', so 'completely' adds nothing.

Not all description is bad. You just need to choose strong adjectives, and use adverbs expressively. Adjectives like 'new', 'simple', or 'unique' can carry valuable meaning or express important benefits. And a little sensory detail goes a long way: a 'juicy steak' sounds tastier than a plain old 'steak' (see 'Make it real' in chapter 11).

In the same way, adverbs can make important distinctions: 'pointlessly carrying on' isn't the same as 'bravely carrying on'. Or they can be the quickest and simplest way to make a point. It's better to say 'instantly recognisable' than 'capable of being recognised in an instant' or something equally clunky.

If you can't put your finger on the right word, by all means use a thesaurus. Some writers say you shouldn't, but it's fine to get a reminder of words you already know – including those that are simpler than what you've got now. What *isn't* OK is a magpie-like quest for obscure, flashy words to use for their own sake.

'Treat adjectives and adverbs as if they cost £500 each,' says top copywriter Tony Brignull. 'But verbs are free.'[60] To apply this test, work through your copy and ask yourself whether you'd pay to keep each one of your adjectives and adverbs. If you would, great. If not, turn them into verbs or just give them the boot.

Get the length right

Have you come across the debate over short copy versus long copy? It can get pretty heated.

Long-copy disciples often praise classic print ads from years gone by, suggesting that writing long copy is a lost art we should revive. Short-copy enthusiasts, on the other hand, point to social platforms like Twitter to suggest that 'microcopy' is more in tune with what modern readers like to write and share.[61]

Reading those arguments, you might think that it's all about progress. Long copy is old-fashioned and short copy is modern; copy just gets shorter and shorter over time. Some marketers even argue that people's attention spans have actually contracted in recent years, and that copy is just shrinking to fit.[62]

---

60 For this and lots more wisdom in under two minutes, see tinyurl.com/ tonybrignull

61 For more on writing for short formats, see *Microstyle: The Art of Writing Little* by Christopher Johnson, W.W. Norton & Company, 2012, and *How to Write Short: Word Craft for Fast Times* by Roy Peter Clark, Little, Brown US, 2014.

62 The statistics on shorter attention spans are widely quoted, but there's little evidence to back them up. See *Busting the attention span myth* by Simon Maybin, BBC, 10 March 2017 (tinyurl.com/attentionmyth).

Actually, if you look around, you'll see that both long and short copy are alive and well. To paraphrase the Howard Luck Gossage quote from chapter 1: people read what interests them, and sometimes it's short. (Or long.)

These days, there are lots of compact digital formats like tweets and GIFs that people like and share in a very visible way. They're even spilling over into the offline world, with things like emojis popping up in print ads. But just because readers get a buzz from short stuff, that doesn't mean they won't quietly enjoy something much longer, or that they're somehow incapable of dealing with it. Yes, people are sharing cat GIFs – but they're also binge-watching *Game of Thrones*. And they like both those things because of their *quality*, not their length. In the same way, the point is not how long or short your copy is, but how *interesting* it is.

As we've seen, your reader's attention is precious, and you should never waste it. People rarely complain that adverts or other marketing materials are too short. And shorter is simpler, which is usually better. But on the other hand, people will read on and on if they're absorbed in a story, learning something useful or simply enjoying the writing. No copy is too long if it can hold the reader's attention right to the end.

From your perspective, your copy needs to be long enough to do its job, but no longer. In chapter 7 ('Give information'), we saw how different readers have different levels of knowledge about products, which can affect how much you need to write. Some readers are ready to buy and just need convincing, which means shorter copy. Others don't even know that the product or anything like it exists, so they need more background. Whatever the reader knows or thinks right now, your copy needs to be long enough to get them from where they are now to where you want them to be.

There might be other times where either longer or shorter copy will work, as alternative ways to tackle the same brief. Let's say you're writing a magazine advert for Scotch whisky. One approach would be to present a simple headline ('A drop of history') and let the imagery do the rest. Another would be to tell the story of the distillery, with all its different characters, places and events. The underlying strategy is the same: emphasise heritage as a guarantee of quality. But the copy length could vary from four words to 400.

The length of the copy can also send a message in itself, regardless of what the words actually say. 'I believe, without any research to support me,' wrote David Ogilvy, 'that advertisements with long copy convey the impression that you have *something important to say*, whether people read the copy or not.'[63] But on the other hand, short copy might give an impression of simplicity, confidence or strength.

The short-copy version of all that: if it's working, it's the right length.

Pace yourself

If you read fiction, you'll already know all about pace. While a thriller might zip along from one event to the next, a romance might linger over descriptions or inner monologues rather than constantly pushing the action forward.

How you pace your copy depends on the effect you want to achieve, and the product experience you want to evoke. For example, if you were writing about a takeaway sandwich shop, you'd probably want to give an impression of brisk, no-nonsense service. But copy for a fine restaurant might have a much more languorous pace, reflecting the more leisurely experience.

You might also want to slow down the pace to create a particular mood. Some charity ads and mailings take time to carefully describe the plight of those they're asking the reader to help. As long as the reader stays interested, this deepens empathy and makes the call for help more powerful.

63 *Ogilvy on Advertising* by David Ogilvy, Prion, 2007, p. 88.

Get rhythm

Rhythm is the pattern of stressed and unstressed syllables in a sequence of words. If you listen to someone talking, you'll hear that they don't just drone on in a monotone. Instead, they put a stress, or emphasis, on certain syllables. You can hear this as a slight increase in loudness, or a longer vowel. You can also hear pauses between words, which in writing are often indicated by punctuation.

When people read, they 'hear' the words in their heads, as if they were listening to someone speaking.[64] So if you want your copy to be convincing and persuasive, it needs to 'sound right' to readers, even though it may never be spoken aloud. And if you want it to sound conversational, it needs to have the same rhythm as everyday speech.

At the most basic level, your copy should have a pleasing pattern of stressed and unstressed syllables. You also want a nice mix of shorter and longer words, and enough pauses to let the reader mentally 'draw breath' between your points.

It usually helps to read your copy aloud, or get someone else (or a text-to-speech app) to read it to you. The rhythm of your words will leap out at you straight away.

When your copy sounds awkward, you'll often find that you're not mixing up the rhythm enough. There are lots of ways to put that right: moving words around, switching between synonyms, changing punctuation, splitting or joining sentences, using or dropping contractions ('don't', 'you've' etc), adding or removing 'that's, and many more.

Here's an example of rhythm that could be improved:

Choose from loads of beautiful patterns, including smart stripes, fun spots and sophisticated Argyll.

64 'How Silent Is Silent Reading? Intracerebral Evidence for Top-Down Activation of Temporal Voice Areas during Reading' by Marcela Perrone-Bertolotti et al., *Journal of Neuroscience*, 5 December 2012, vol. 32(49) pp. 17554–17562

Can you hear what's wrong? 'Choose from loads of' is too regular, with four monosyllabic words in a row, while 'smart stripes' and 'fun spots' both jam two stresses right up next to each other. On the other hand, 'sophisticated Argyll' has too many unstressed syllables in a row, making the rhythm sound stretched out.

With just a few little tweaks that don't affect the meaning, we can get a much more balanced, flowing rhythm (changes underlined):

> Choose from <u>dozens</u> of beautiful patterns, including <u>snazzy</u> stripes, <u>funky</u> spots and <u>classy</u> Argyll.

The next level up is the rhythm of sentences. As with words, you want a mix of short and long, so the rhythm doesn't become too regular and put your reader to sleep. Short sentences can be just one or two words, while longer ones should fit within a single breath, like a line from a song. If your sentence gets any longer than that, you're probably asking it to do the job of two or more shorter ones. Find a way to split it up.

Finally, there's the rhythm of paragraphs. Each one should develop a single idea. When you break between paragraphs, you're telling the reader that you've finished making a point, so they should pause, reflect and mentally draw breath before carrying on. If you put your breaks in the wrong place, they'll have to stop in the middle of an idea, which is disconcerting. And if you don't use enough breaks, they'll start to feel overwhelmed.

You can use this 'stop and think' effect to make an important point really stand out, by placing it in a short, one-sentence paragraph. It's like a slap round the face that makes the reader sit up and take notice.

See for yourself.

Don't overuse this technique, or you'll cheapen the effect and drive your reader round the bend. Short works.

But not too much. It wears people out. Hurts their heads. Like this. See? So don't.

Make it rhyme

At the moment, the fashion in copywriting is for casual conversational language or abstract taglines. Jaunty rhyming slogans are off the menu. That's a shame, because rhymes can be very powerful – psychologists have even found that people see rhyming statements as being 22% more accurate than non-rhyming ones.[65] Because rhymes are easier to understand, people feel they're more true.

One modern rhyming slogan is the one Tesco used for its home delivery service:

> You shop, we drop.

The rhyme is snappy and memorable, but it also strengthens the message. The two rhyming words reflect the division of labour, which is the main benefit: you do your shopping online, and we'll do the grunt work of getting it home. Tesco's slogan was so strong that Asda responded with its own version:

> From our store to your door.

This vintage slogan for Ariel (P&G), the washing powder, did something similar:

> When the stain says hot, but the label says not.

Again, the rhyme made the message more powerful, because it emphasised the tension between the need for a high-temperature wash ('hot') and the restrictive washing instructions ('not'). Obviously, the way to resolve that tension was to buy Ariel.

---

65 'Birds of a Feather Flock Conjointly (?): Rhyme as Reason in Aphorisms' by Matthew S. McGlone and Jessica Tofighbakhsh, *Psychological Science*, 1 September 2000. Cited in 'Is Rhyme Past Its Prime?' by Richard Shotton, *The Drum*, 22 July 2017.

Add alliteration

Alliteration means using words that start with the same sound. Like rhyme, it's a way to give your copy more clout. Unlike rhyme, though, you can use it (sparingly) in body copy to underline particularly pertinent points without the effect jumping out at the reader.

As with rhyme, the best alliteration links words and ideas to say something about a benefit, like this classic slogan for Double Diamond beer (Ind Coope/Molson Coors):

A Double Diamond Works Wonders

This takes the alliteration that's already in the brand name and combines it with another two-word phrase to give a nicely balanced result. (The line was a victim of its own success: it ran for so long that it eventually morphed into 'A Double Diamond *Still* Works Wonders', which isn't nearly as pleasing.)

The same technique still works today, as in this slogan for Lucozade energy drink…

Show Busy Who's Boss

…and this one for Nerf toy guns (Hasbro):

It's Nerf or Nothin'

In just four words, this line sets up an opposition between two extremes, making the competition irrelevant. Kids can remember it and repeat it later – not least to their parents, who will appreciate all too well that this is the statement of an expensive but highly desirable market leader.

Make it punchy

We saw in chapter 6 how commands can make headlines more direct. You can use the same technique throughout your copy, particularly when you want to make benefits more punchy.

For example, here's a description of a B2B benefit, for customer relationship management software:

> *C-Base* lets you view all your customers by industry segment, lifetime value and share of wallet, so you can target your marketing to those with the highest sales potential.

B2B copy often ends up peppered with phrases like 'lets you', 'so you can' and 'helps you to', to link technical features to business benefits. You can avoid that by framing benefits as commands:

> View all customers by industry segment, lifetime value and share of wallet. Target marketing to those with the highest sales potential.

Go one step further and you can make your copy even punchier – if you don't mind breaking a few rules. For example, you could go from this:

> See all your customer data in one place.
> View full details with one click.

To this:

> All your customer data in one place.
> One-click detail views.

These are no longer command sentences, but verb-less fragments, a bit like bullet points within text. They may not be strictly grammatical, but they *are* crystal clear, and very punchy. Sometimes, that's a trade worth making – particularly online, when readers are skim-reading and clicking around rather than dutifully working through every word.

Break the rules

Should you aim for accurate spelling and grammar? Definitely. But if following the rules would make your copy less effective, it's better to break them.

No top copywriter would throw out a great idea because it involved a spelling or grammar 'mistake'. If they did, Heinz might have ended up with this:

Beans Mean Heinz

Instead of the famous:

Beanz Meanz Heinz

That slogan wasn't written by a six-year-old, but by an experienced creative director (Maurice Drake) at the top of his game. The point is that it's OK to break the rules, as long as you do it knowingly, and with good reason. There's a big difference between leaving in careless mistakes and making a conscious decision to bend the rules for greater impact.

When you know the rules, you have a better idea of when and how to break them. For example, confusing 'you're' and 'your' looks pretty bad and is unlikely to improve your copy. But starting a sentence with a conjunction ('but', 'and', etc), while often regarded as technically incorrect, adds a lot of punch and will go completely unnoticed by everyone apart from grammar and punctuation nerds.[66]

As author Neil Gaiman says, 'Don't obsess over grammar. If you have to obsess, obsess over clarity. Write as clearly as you can.' That's very good advice for a copywriter. If you have to choose between being clear and being correct, be clear.

---

66 For a lively guide to punctuation, see *Eats, Shoots and Leaves* by Lynne Truss, Fourth Estate, 2009. For a reference book, see *New Hart's Rules: The Oxford Style Guide*, OUP, 2014.

Check it... or get it checked

The longer you work on a piece of copy, the harder it becomes to spot mistakes in it. While the client might pick up on errors themselves, it's not really their job, and you certainly shouldn't rely on them to do it. It's up to you to check your work as carefully as you can.

As a minimum, print your copy out and read it off paper. This is much more accurate than trying to work off a screen. Choose a clear, readable typeface and make it big (at least 12pt) with plenty of line spacing (at least 16pt). If you can, leave some time between writing and checking, so you come back to your copy with fresh eyes.

Even better, get someone else to proofread your copy – preferably, someone who's never seen it before. Most freelance proofreaders offer very reasonable rates, and will give you the reassurance of a professional look over your copy. For longer projects, they'll help you make sure that things like punctuation, abbreviations and specialised words are used consistently throughout. And they may also suggest ideas for improvement.

TRY THIS

Under the microscope

One of the best ways to learn is by looking really closely at other people's writing. Choose something you like and analyse what makes it work. Or look at something you *don't* like, and think how you'd improve it.

13

BE **PERSUASIVE**

Use six proven principles to make your copy more persuasive.

Taking the first step: a persuasion story

Tim and Olly are both in their 40s. Tim likes to keep in shape, but Olly is more of a real-ale, full-English-breakfast sort of guy. Privately, Tim thinks Olly's been letting himself go, and could definitely stand to lose a pound or two. Olly doesn't see why he can't enjoy the things he likes without being guilt-tripped.

One day, Tim buys a wearable fitness tracker. Obviously, he loves it. But he thinks it could be good for Olly too. Could he persuade him to give it a try?

One Sunday, after his morning miles, Tim makes his move.

'This tracker's great,' he tells Olly breathlessly. 'It really motivates you to keep fit, and you could lose weight with it too. I feel great since I started using it, and people are saying I look slimmer.'

Without looking up from his Sunday paper, Olly grunts noncommittally. This doesn't sound like a conversation that ends in a roast dinner.

Tim tries a different tack.

'Everyone's using them,' he points out. 'Just about every person I see in the park has one.'

'Well, I'm not everyone,' says Olly, with a pout.

'Dave's got one,' says Tim. 'You know Dave, with Daisy the beagle?'

'Don't tell me. Daisy's got one too, right?' retorts Olly, sarcastically.

'His doctor told him to get one,' explains Tim. 'After his health check. His blood pressure was off the chart.'

'There's nothing wrong with me,' insists Olly, shifting uneasily in his armchair. 'My grandad lived to 100, and he never had a robot on his wrist telling him to take the stairs.'

'I got £40 off mine in the John Lewis sale,' says Tim. 'There's probably still a few left.'

'I might have a look next time I'm in,' concedes Olly, grudgingly.

'Well, we did say we'd turn over a new leaf in January,' points out Tim. 'The morning after Helen's party, remember? I'm making an effort, so it's the least you can do.'

'Oh, go on then,' says Olly. 'I'll give it a go. But you still won't catch me wearing it to the pub.'

The power of persuasion

In the story, Tim starts off by pointing out the benefits of his tracker, both tangible (keep fit, lose weight) and intangible (look better, feel good). But Olly doesn't really need Tim to tell him about fitness trackers and what they do. Even though he knows that having one would probably benefit him, he's still not ready to try one.

Describing benefits isn't enough to persuade Olly. What's holding him back isn't lack of information, but his own thoughts, beliefs and feelings.

Like all of us, Olly doesn't really want to change. He wants to stay right where he is, sitting in his comfort zone, doing what he's always done. Staying the same is safe and reassuring, but change is risky and unsettling. So Tim has to make all the running, and show Olly why what he's suggesting will be better than simply doing nothing.

It's easy to think of persuasion as making someone do something against their will – *pushing* them over the bridge from chapter 1. But that's coercion or blackmail, not persuasion. No copywriter can make a reader do something they really don't want to do. (If the reader would *never* buy the product, they wouldn't be one of the target customers you identified in chapter 4.)

To persuade the reader, you must carefully choose arguments that tip their emotional balance, so that the benefits of acting on your message outweigh the benefits of ignoring it. Once you've done that, the reader's thoughts and feelings will be aligned, and they'll be ready to act on your message.

Persuasion with purpose

Persuasion works best when it's aimed at a simple, clearly defined outcome. Tim isn't trying to convert Olly into a fitness fanatic during this one conversation. He just wants him to try wearing a fitness tracker. If that happens, Tim will have succeeded.

In the same way, your persuasive copy doesn't have to transform the reader's worldview. It just has to get them to take the action you identified in chapter 4 – which is usually trying a product or contacting a firm. For that to happen, the reader doesn't necessarily have to accept every last claim you make, or share all the values of the brand. They just have to believe that the product will offer them value.

If the reader's ideas and attitudes change at all, it will probably happen later on, when they actually use the product. Think of your own experience: your deepest beliefs usually come from things you've lived, rather than things you've heard or read.

Six principles of persuasion

Social proof
We do what other people do

Liking
We listen more to
people we like

Authority
We obey people we respect

Scarcity
The less there is,
the more we want it

Consistency
We honour our past
commitments

Reciprocity
We return favours
and pay debts

Robert B. Cialdini's six principles of persuasion

Six principles of persuasion

Tim brings Olly round by using six principles of persuasion: social proof, liking, authority, scarcity, consistency and reciprocity (in that order). They're taken from the work of management researcher and writer Robert B. Cialdini, who spent decades researching what makes some people better at persuasion than others.[67] Let's look at each one in turn.

Social proof

When Tim tells Olly that 'everyone' is using fitness trackers, he's using the principle of social proof.

Social proof works because human beings don't like standing out. We decide how to behave by following cues from the people around us.

The strongest cues come from our colleagues, friends and family. But we also respond to more general cues, like fashions we read about in magazines or trending topics on social media.

As a copywriter, you can't create peer cues. People will find those for themselves when they chat to friends or check Facebook. However, you can suggest that there are popular trends and preferences out there that readers 'should' be following. Your basic argument is, 'Lots of other people are doing this, so you should too.' Here's how Betterware uses the technique:

7 million people can't be wrong

Last year they followed these 3 SIMPLE STEPS to easier shopping...

The less certain we are about something, the more powerful social proof becomes. When we don't know much about a situation ourselves, we assume that other people

---

67 *Influence: The Psychology of Persuasion* by Robert B. Cialdini, Harper Business, 2006.

must know more, so we follow them. That's why many apps, ecommerce sites and 'software as a service' firms offer a mid-priced 'most popular' option, reassuring people that it's the 'right' one to choose. It also makes social proof particularly useful if you're targeting readers who are unfamiliar with a market, like first-time homebuyers, young learner drivers or people taking up a new hobby.

Brands with a strong market share are very well placed to use social proof, as shown by this line for Whiskas® (Mars®):

Eight out of ten owners said their cats preferred it.

The social group is very clear – cat owners – and the statistic is impressive. Exactly what the cats preferred Whiskas® *to* isn't made clear, but that doesn't matter, because most readers will never dig that deep. If you're a first-time kitten owner wondering what Snuggles might like for tea, the popular choice seems a safe place to start.

We tend to give even more weight to social proof when we know about multiple sources that all agree. The more different voices or perspectives we hear supporting a course of action, the more likely we are to take it. That's why Whiskas®' TV ads featured several different cat owners, all saying slightly different but unanimously positive things.

You can still use social proof if you're not writing for a leading brand, as long as you choose the right frame of reference:

Vanguard is the choice of thousands of van owners throughout the UK.

There's no need to get into whether 'thousands' actually represents that big a proportion of UK van owners. The reader will still get the impression that lots of them choose *Vanguard*.

We follow social cues from people who are generally similar to us. When Tim tells Olly that 'everyone' has a tracker, he doesn't mean everyone in the world, but lots of people who are in their social circle, or could be. So it's important to be clear about what social group you're referring to, and consider whether readers will identify with them. You could even encourage the reader to make the connection themselves:

> Hundreds of homeowners in your situation have already made the switch.

Social proof appeals to the reader's self-interest indirectly, by showing how others are benefiting from the product. But that doesn't always work if someone other than the reader would benefit from a 'sale' – for example, when good causes are appealing for help.

In their book *Think Small*,[68] Owain Service and Rory Gallagher present this copy, which was used by the UK government's gov.uk site to encourage people to sign up for the NHS Organ Donor Register:

> Every day thousands of people who see this page decide to register.

When this copy was tested, it actually *reduced* signups, because it gave readers a reason *not* to act. They thought, 'If thousands of others are helping, maybe I don't need to.' A better approach might be to use scarcity (see below) to emphasise how *few* people are registering. Instead of suggesting that the reader themselves will lose out by not acting, that would tell them that *other people* will lose out if the reader fails to act.

---

68 *Think Small: The Surprisingly Simple Ways to Reach Big Goals* by Owain Service and Rory Gallagher, Michael O' Mara Books, 2017.

Liking

When Tim points out to Olly that their mutual friend already has a fitness tracker, he's appealing to Olly's liking for Dave (and possibly Daisy the beagle too).

We listen to the views of people we like. That's why we're far more likely to follow product recommendations from our friends or family. It's also why we react against pushy, obnoxious salespeople, even if they're offering us some benefit.

Robert Cialdini used the example of Tupperware parties to illustrate liking. The product may have been new and unfamiliar, but because guests already knew and liked their Tupperware host, they were far more likely to buy from them.

The problem is, your copy *isn't* known and liked. Your reader's never seen it before, and it's getting in their face with a message they never asked for. Plus they may never have heard of the brand that's 'speaking'. Far from being a supportive friend, you're a cognitive mugger, hijacking the reader's attention for your own ends. So how can you use the principle of liking?

One way is through borrowed interest, which we saw in chapter 9. An endorsement from a celebrity or a reference to a favourite film is a shortcut to liking that might rub off on your product.

Another way is through customer testimonials and reviews. If the reader warms to the people who are 'talking' about the product, they're more likely to believe them. In this case, liking works in tandem with social proof.

If neither of those is possible, you can try to show the reader you understand their situation. If you build empathy before you start pushing benefits, they might like the brand or product a little more.

Here's some copy from Boots, the UK pharmacy chain. It appeared on the envelope that customers received their photo prints in:

> At Boots, we know how precious your memories are. That's why our experts only use the highest quality materials before carefully hand-checking every photo.

Here, the underlying logic is: 'We understand you, which is why we take these quality steps. Don't you like us, and our service?'

Another approach is to say something nice about the reader:

> As a parent, you already know all about managing your time, ending arguments and juggling priorities. Now there's a way to have one less thing to worry about...

If this works, you'll get a little mental nod of agreement from the reader, and maybe a spark of emotion too. But as in real life, empathic statements must sound both sincere and credible, or the reader will see through them. Also, as we saw in chapter 7 ('Give information'), you could just irritate the reader by telling them things they already know. Maybe the best way to be liked is to get right to the point, and waste as little of the reader's time as you can.

Authority

When Tim mentions Dave's doctor advising him to improve his fitness, he's using the principle of authority.

We tend to obey people in authority, particularly when we're not sure what to do. Many people can exercise authority: parents, teachers, politicians, celebrities, policemen, bosses, scientists and experts in any field. Their authority can flow from their superior knowledge, their official rank or qualifications, an endorsement from someone else or just their own character. Organisations, publications and brands can have authority, as well as people.

Whatever form authority takes, it's always a two-way street: it only works because someone accepts it, or submits to it. So if you want to invoke an authority figure, it must be one who actually has authority in the eyes of your reader.

Tim's tactic works well because the authority of Dave's doctor could easily extend to Olly. Clearly, Dave's a middle-aged guy who needs to watch his weight, just like Olly. If Dave had been in his 70s, Olly might have argued that the doctor's advice didn't apply to him.

It's a lot easier if the reader has already heard of the authority, without you having to tell them. If they probably haven't heard of them, you'll have to decide whether the authority will be convincing enough at first sight. Or, if you're writing in the first person, you may have to establish your own authority, which could mean calling on other sources of authority to back up your own.

Authority is often used in ads for cosmetics and healthcare products like shampoo, toothpaste and face cream. On TV, there'll be a 'science bit', possibly featuring an actual scientist or doctor in a white coat, backing up the product's claims with impressive-sounding facts and figures.

At other times, authority can be more intangible. In the 1970s, Brut 33 wanted to persuade men to start wearing aftershave. So they recruited Henry Cooper, a British boxer, to appear in their ads. Seeing the ultra-butch Cooper 'splash it all over' gave men permission to do the same, because he was an 'authority' on masculinity.

Wherever your authority comes from, give it confidence with simple, concrete language and positive statements (as we saw in chapter 11). An authority that sounds unsure of itself won't convince anyone.

Scarcity

When Tim mentions that he got his tracker in the John Lewis sale, he's invoking the principle of scarcity. This says that we value something more if it's in short supply, and less if it's plentiful.

Think about the box of thin mints you get at Christmas. You scoff the first few without a care, and even offer them round to your guests, safe in the knowledge that there are plenty more left. Before you know it, you're down to the very last one. And it somehow seems more precious and delicious than any of the others you so merrily munched, all those minutes ago.

The more abundant things are, the more freedom of choice we have. As they become more and more scarce, we gradually lose that freedom. We hate to lose freedoms that we already enjoy, so we react by grabbing and holding on to scarce things, hoarding whatever freedom we have left.

Scarcity activates our natural fear of making the wrong choice. As things become more scarce, we start to worry about the opportunity 'getting away', and imagine how sad we'll feel if it does. If that feeling is strong enough, we might buy purely to prevent future regret, as a sort of emotional insurance. It's not that we necessarily need the product; we just don't want to regret not buying it. If you've ever staggere home from the January sales laden with bags of stuff you didn't really need, you've seen this effect at first hand.

You can use scarcity by making your product seem scarce in one or more ways.

The first, and simplest, is quantity. If there's only a limited amount or number of the product, people will see it as more valuable:

> Just 500 of these beautiful limited edition *Star Trek* commemorative plates have been produced.

Next is time: readers only have a limited period to make a purchase or take up an offer. Here's an easyJet ad that uses time scarcity:

> Up to 25% off.
> Every seat, every route, every day.
> Hurry, sale ends midnight Tuesday!

Then there's competition. Not only is the offer limited, but others may get there first:

> Demand for this prestigious conference is sure to be strong. Act now to book your Early Bird ticket before the May 30 deadline.

Exclusivity flatters readers that they are part of a select group who are being given a unique opportunity. Readers 'should' take up the offer because it's especially for them:

> As someone who's previously bought *Lawnmower World*, you've been selected to receive details of this incredible subscription offer...

Lastly, there's invitation, which comes into play with 'refer a friend' schemes and similar. It's like exclusivity, but this time the offer is aimed at the individual reader personally, not just a group they belong to. Spotify used this technique to build demand, interest and user commitment in the early days of its rollout:

> Spotify Free is currently in an invitation-only beta, which means you need to have received an invitation token to access the service.

Scarcity often features in calls to action (see chapter 8), when you need to impress on readers that they must act *now*, not just sometime in the future.

A final thought: the scarcity doesn't have to be real. You could create it artificially, either by suggesting changes to the way the product is actually sold, or just by making it sound scarce in your copy. For instance, since each new Spotify invitee was given another 10 invitations to hand out, the number of invitations was actually infinite. But the 'invitation only' positioning made the service feel exclusive and exciting nonetheless.

Consistency

When Tim reminds Olly that they've both decided to get healthier, he's using the principle of consistency.

Once we've made a commitment, we tend to stick with it. That's because we want to feel consistent and honest, and appear that way to other people too. Breaking a commitment, on the other hand, suggests that we're unreliable or untrustworthy.

A simple use of consistency is to 'cross-sell' one product based on the reader's liking for another. Here's how Hellmann's (Unilever) did it:

> If you like Hellmann's, you'll love these!

Or you can 'up-sell' the reader to a bigger or better option by suggesting it's a natural progression:

> Admit it. You've taken that consumer camera as far as you can. It's time to upgrade to your first digital SLR from *CamCo*.

This 'in for a penny, in for a pound' angle suggests that the reader needs to make another purchase to continue a journey they've already begun. The implication is that if they *don't* make it, they're standing still – or even going backwards.

You could also point to a commitment that the reader may well have made, or seriously considered:

> Our pay-and-play gym sessions make it easy to keep your New Year's resolutions with no big commitments.

If you're writing for a reader who you know has made a concrete commitment, consistency is a great way to encourage them to stick with it:

Thanks for subscribing to *Copywriting World*.

We're sure you've gained a wealth of ideas and insights over the last 12 months. To continue your learning journey, renew your subscription today and get three issues completely free.

Here, the underlying logic is that you subscribed and enjoyed the magazine, so it would be inconsistent not to carry on.

In chapter 6, we saw how questions can get the reader involved, and get them to say a mental 'yes' that prepares the ground for your message:

Would you like to earn more interest on your savings?

Since the product obviously offers a high interest rate, ignoring it is inconsistent with the reader's answer to this question.

Another approach is to ask a question linked to a purchase, in a tactic beloved of US infomercials:

How much would you pay for a round-the-world cruise?

This has two effects. First, it uses what salespeople call an 'assumptive close'. Even if the reader's never considered a cruise before, the question makes the purchase a done deal; only the price is up for discussion. Second, they're prompted to start thinking about what they'd pay for it. If they find out later that the actual price is lower than that, their price objections are weakened because they've already 'agreed' to pay more.

You can also use consistency to appeal to the reader's morals. A charity 'mugger' for the RSPCA once approached me and asked if I was an animal lover. I answered 'yes,' as most people probably would. But what looked like a casual question turned out to be a clever consistency play: the next question was whether I'd help suffering animals by donating. Since I'd just said that I loved animals, saying no felt like breaking a promise.

The MPAA's anti-piracy video ad, included on DVDs, used consistency to persuade the reader *not* to do something:

> You wouldn't steal a car.
> You wouldn't steal a handbag.
> You wouldn't steal a television.
> You wouldn't steal a movie.
>
> Downloading pirated films is stealing.
> Stealing is against the law.
>
> Piracy. It's a crime.

Incidentally, consistency is one reason why brands are so keen on people posting reviews online. Obviously, user reviews help attract new customers (through social proof). But they also convince the reviewers themselves. Commitments that are written down are far more powerful – so by writing about a positive experience, or why they'd buy again, reviewers are turning the principle of consistency on themselves.

Reciprocity

'I'm making an effort,' says Tim, 'so it's the least you can do.' By offering Olly this quid pro quo, he's appealing to the principle of reciprocity, which says that people tend to return a favour. Because Tim's been getting his steps in so diligently, he argues, Olly owes him a few miles in return. It's only fair, after all.

Reciprocity is about giving people something of value, so they feel that they owe you something. Then you ask them to act as a way to repay their 'debt'.

Reciprocity is why marketers are happy to throw free stuff at consumers. A free sample isn't just a way to try a product; it makes people feel they owe the brand a purchase. A free biro in a charity mailing is more than a branded gift; it hangs around people's homes, guilt-tripping them into donating, because it feels too valuable to simply throw away. B2B firms offer free consultancy to give potential clients a taste of their service, or produce glossy promotional books to sit on their bookshelves. Even if these tactics don't bring in a sale straight away, they still 'warm up' the reader and form some sort of bond with them.

What can copywriting, on its own, give the reader? Well, if it's interesting and creative enough, it can give them entertainment value, an emotional kick or the satisfaction of having puzzled out a meaning. That feeling may be slight and fleeting, but it's there.

Longer, more detailed copy can give people something more substantial. That's the idea behind content marketing. You give the reader valuable knowledge or advice in the form of a subject introduction or how-to guide. In return, they give you their email address, but they also form an impression of your brand as being helpful, knowledgeable and impartial. Then, when the time comes for them to buy, they remember you and get in touch. Writing a 20-page white paper might seem a lot of effort in return for a few phone calls or email enquiries – but if you're selling something high-value like management consultancy, every lead is gold.

At the time, Olly probably thought Tim's running was for Tim's own enjoyment, and not really anything to do with him. But Tim deftly reframes it as a sort of investment into their mutual health that Olly needs to match. In the same way, you may have to point out to the reader that they've received something of value. One way is to put a nominal value on a giveaway, such as 'a free consultancy worth £100'. If that's not plausible, you can simply emphasise the size or value of the gift – for example, 'a comprehensive 20-page buyer's guide written by our insurance experts'.

Bring it all together

We've looked at the six persuasive techniques in isolation. But as Tim and Olly's story shows, it's often more powerful to combine them, or use them in sequence. Here's an example:

> You've probably heard how important it is to make a will. Maybe your friends have already done it. Most financial advisors agree: if you want to care for your family after you're gone, it's never too early to sort out your legacy. We'll give you all the help and advice you need to make a will that's right for you – and all for a tiny fraction of the gift you want to leave. Give us a ring to book your free consultation.

Before you read on, see if you can identify which persuasive techniques this copy uses.

The first sentence uses social proof: if you've already heard about it, lots of people must be doing it. The second adds in liking, inviting the reader to think about people they know, and what they've done. 'Most financial advisors' invokes authority, while 'care for your family' implies that making a will is consistent with an aim that most people share. 'It's never too early' gently reminds the reader that they may have less time to act than they think, invoking scarcity. Comparing the fee with the total value of the inheritance helps to overcome the 'too expensive' objection by reframing the cost as insignificant in context (see 'Reframe costs' in chapter 14). Finally, the promises of 'help and advice' and a 'free consultation' set up reciprocity by offering something of value upfront.[69]

---

69 For more on writing persuasively (not just in copy), see *Can I Change Your Mind?* by Lindsay Camp, A&C Black, 2007.

Overcoming objections

In the film *Boiler Room* (2000), Jim Young (played by Ben Affleck) delivers a fiery pep talk to a group of young traders who sell penny stocks by cold calling. He tells them:

> There is no such thing as a no-sale call. A sale is made on every call you make. Either you sell the client some stock, or he sells you on a reason he can't.

The point is that negotiation is a two-way street. You're always persuading *somebody*, and they have an agenda too – even if it's just to do nothing, or to carry on as they are. (Psychologists call this attachment to the way things are 'status quo bias'.)

Think back to chapter 4. There are things the reader wants to do and have, and other things they want to get rid of. Some desires will match up with the benefits you're offering, which helps you. But others could become objections you need to overcome. For example, if you're selling an essential like washing-up liquid, your reader will be using a rival brand already. So you need to persuade them to stop using it, if only for a week, to give yours a try.

Many objections are rooted in fear. Not nameless terrors or screaming phobias, but the nagging anxieties that buzz around our heads all day. The fear of being found out, disapproval or ridicule. The fear of making a mistake or being ripped off. The fear of change, and an unknowable future.

Seen in this light, it's clear that your job as a persuader isn't to bully or manipulate the reader, but to *reassure* them. They're ready to step on to the bridge; you just have to convince them that everything will be all right when they do. That's what Don Draper of *Mad Men* means when he says that happiness is a billboard saying 'You are OK'. Whatever you're selling, you're *always* selling peace of mind.

Here are a few common objections, in both their B2C and B2B forms, with suggestions on how to overcome them.

Objection		How to overcome it
B2C form	**B2B form**	
I don't need it	This isn't relevant to our needs	Use consistency to show that this buying decision is in line with other decisions the reader has already made
		Use social proof and/or liking to show that others are using the product and benefiting from it
		Turn 'don't need' into 'want' by cultivating desire
		Make the experience real to take the reader forward in time, beyond their purchasing decision (see 'Make it real' in chapter 11)
I've already got one	We already use something similar that meets our needs	Give specific information to quantify advantages over competing products (or earlier versions of yours)
		Use social proof to show that others used to feel that way too – but changed their minds
I can't afford it / It's too expensive	We don't have the budget for it / The upfront investment is too high	Use anchoring or reframing to put the cost in a different perspective (see 'Reframe costs' in chapter 14)
		Use social proof to show that other, similar people/firms are buying the product
		Use consistency to show that if you can afford A, you can definitely afford B
I don't believe it will work (for me)	It's unproven/unsuitable	Use social proof in the form of customer testimonials
		Use authority in the form of an expert review or endorsement

I can't be bothered	The opportunity cost and management overhead are too great	Use reciprocity: do something for the reader, or give them something, so they feel obliged to do something in return
		Show that it's quick and easy (see chapter 8)
I'll do it later	We can't consider an investment like this right now	Use scarcity to exert time pressure
		Use consistency to link an immediate purchase with another goal or commitment the reader might have ('if you want to do A, the first step is B')
		Use social proof to say that others have already bought

There may also be specific objections that you know readers are likely to raise, based on your research or what the client tells you. The sign created by Norwich's Assembly House (see opposite) includes two examples: 'Worth the walk' counters the objection that the venue is too far from the city centre, while 'Casual dress welcome' reassures readers that it's not too posh for them.

This example shows that objections needn't be rational, or based in fact. In reality, the Assembly House is very central, and has never had a dress code. But preconceptions about these things could still make people think twice about visiting. We worry about lots of things, most of which never happen.

Norwich's Assembly House addresses two reader objections:
'It's too far away' and 'It's too posh'.
REPRODUCED BY KIND PERMISSION OF THE ASSEMBLY HOUSE

TRY THIS

Persuade yourself

Think of something you really should do, but have been putting off. It could be getting some insurance, sorting out your clothes, painting your window frames or anything else. Now see if you can persuade yourself to do it using the techniques you've learned this chapter.

14

USE **PSYCHOLOGY**

Work with readers' natural cognitive biases and
distortions to change their point of view.

___

It's all in the mind

We humans are pretty bad at knowing the truth. In fact, our
brains suffer from so many distortions, omissions and biases
that our perceptions can be completely at odds with reality.
We're particularly hopeless when it comes to comparing
things like cost, probability and size. But the good news is
that you can exploit these loopholes to give your copy some
extra traction.

Now, you might feel that some of these approaches cross the
line from persuasion into manipulation. I'm just presenting
them as options. Whether you use them is up to you.

The endowment effect

The endowment effect is the tendency to overvalue things
we already own. If you've ever tried clearing out your
garage or attic, you might have felt this effect in action. You
haven't touched that old stuff in years, and you certainly
wouldn't buy it again today. But because it's *your* stuff, it's
hard to let it go.

Here's an example based on that exact situation:

Moving home? Short of space?

Don't throw out those treasured possessions. Store them securely at *Big Shed* until you can enjoy them again.

Free product samples, time-limited trials, test drives and free-to-play videogames all play on the endowment effect. Once people experience something and become attached to it, they feel it's already theirs. They may not have paid for it, but they have invested their time and attention, which can be just as valuable. Once they've done that, they're more likely to pay real money to keep hold of it.

Loss aversion

Psychologists have found that we prefer avoiding losses to getting gains of the same value.[70] In other words, we hate to lose more than we love to win.

To play on loss aversion, make liberal use of 'your' to emphasise what the reader already has, while pointing out that they could lose it, like this online ad by Squarespace:

Get your domain before it's gone

Get it now

Here, 'your domain' is just a domain that the reader might want. It doesn't even exist until they register it. But the threat that someone else will get there first can still feel like a potential loss. ('Before it's gone' also brings in time scarcity, which we saw in chapter 13.)

---

70 See *Thinking, Fast and Slow* by Daniel Kahneman, Penguin, 2012, pp. 282–286 and elsewhere.

The Forer effect

Psychologist Bertram Forer gave a group of students a personal profile made up of 13 statements and asked them to say how accurate it was. In fact, the 'profile' was exactly the same for all of them. But they still rated the list 4.26/5 for accuracy, on average.[71]

The statements clicked with the students because they were so vague that almost *anyone* could identify with them. For example:

> You have a great need for other people to like and admire you.

> You have a tendency to be critical of yourself.

> At times you have serious doubts as to whether you have made the right decision or done the right thing.

Forer found that the most universal statements began 'At times…'. That's because we don't feel and act exactly the same way in every situation, with our emotions set in stone. Instead, we're constantly moving through different emotional *states*.

In chapter 4, we saw how important it is to empathise with the reader. The Forer effect suggests that the best way to do that might be to talk about something they've probably thought or felt *at some point*. For example:

> From time to time, we all buy clothes that never get worn. Our online personal shopper helps you avoid expensive mistakes.

71 'The Fallacy of Personal Validation: A Classroom Demonstration of Gullibility' by Bertram R. Forer, *Journal of Abnormal and Social Psychology* (American Psychological Association), vol. 44(1): 1959, pp. 118–123.

Or:

> Do you sometimes wonder if you're really saving enough for retirement? Use our simple annuity calculator to see what income you can expect.

To trigger the Forer effect, talk about thoughts and emotions the reader might have, using modifiers like 'sometimes', 'occasionally', 'from time to time', 'now and then', 'probably' and so on. Without these words, your statements might sound too blunt – take them out of the examples above and see.

Reframe costs

In chapter 9, we looked at how to reframe benefits for a creative effect. You can also use reframing to show the cost of the product in a different context, or from a different perspective. This helps to overcome the reader's price objections – thoughts like 'I can't afford it' or 'It's just too expensive'.

If you just come right out with the price of a product, the reader will immediately compare it with zero, which is the 'cost' of not buying it at all. But if you say some other number first, your reader will compare every other number they hear soon afterwards with that. This is called 'anchoring', because it anchors their expectations in a certain range. So if you mention a high price before stating the actual price of the product, readers will think it sounds low:

> While a high-end lawnmower can cost well over £600, the *MerryMo* comes in at a trim £295.

The 'anchor' number can be almost anything, as long as it's relevant (and not an outright lie). It's not really there for information – just to pull the reader's perceptions upwards.

Bigness bias, which is closely related to anchoring, is when smaller amounts sound less significant next to larger amounts. B2B service providers often use it to put their fees in a particular commercial perspective. For example, here's an angle that an information security consultant might take:

> Our information security healthcheck costs just £995. That's a small price to pay for peace of mind when a data breach could land you with a heavy fine, severe reputational damage and thousands of lost sales.

Here, the reader fills in the big number for themselves, by mentally working out what 'thousands' of lost sales would come to, or the financial impact of 'reputational damage'. As long as the amount they come up with is a lot higher than £995, the copy works. (If it isn't, their business is probably too small to use the service anyway.)

Another very popular technique is to compare the price with something the reader feels is affordable, because they've almost certainly bought it:

> For the price of a cup of coffee each week, you could provide clean drinking water for a family in Africa.

This combines bigness bias and consistency (from chapter 13). Bigness bias tells the reader 'This isn't a big cost in terms of your weekly spending', while consistency says 'You're happy to pay for that other affordable thing, so how about this one too?'

You can also encourage the reader to think about costs and benefits more broadly, or over a longer timeframe. Accountants call this 'whole-life cost' or 'total cost of ownership'.

> The *MerryMo* is engineered from high-quality steel parts, so it'll keep on cutting for years, giving you many more mows for your money.

This reminds the reader that spare parts and maintenance are part of the cost of owning a mower, encouraging them to think about it as a long-term investment rather than a one-off cost.

You can divide whole-life costs into tiny fractions, using the familiar but very effective 'pennies per day' technique:

> For as little as £2.50 a day, you can have a fully functioning VOIP exchange for your small office, complete with five phone numbers for dialling in or out.

Finally, you can point to other types of cost saving that offset the price of the product:

> The *InstaHot* water boiler makes a cuppa in seconds rather than minutes, so your team spend less time waiting for the kettle to boil. Over its lifetime, *InstaHot* will pay for itself many times over in energy savings and productivity gains.

Sunk costs

A sunk cost is money that we've spent and can't get back. We tend to honour sunk costs even when it would make more sense to forget them and move on, because we feel we'd be 'wasting' the money we spent before if we did.

Imagine you book a theatre ticket in advance, then fall ill on the day of the performance. You might honour the sunk cost by going to the show even if it makes you feel worse, to avoid 'wasting' the cost of the ticket. In fact, the money is gone no matter what you do, and you'd probably feel better if you stayed in.

You can use sunk costs to promote a product that lets people get more value from something they've already bought. For example:

If you've invested in high-quality tiles, give them
a new lease of life with *Tile-o-Paint*, the cheaper
alternative to retiling.

Reactance

If you've ever tried to get a small child ready to leave the
house, you already know about reactance. It's the tendency
to do the opposite of what we're told, even when it would
benefit us to comply.

Reactance plays a big part in political campaigning.
If a party can position their policies as a rebellion against
somebody – Brussels bureaucrats, the liberal elite, corporate
fat cats – they can turn a vote for them into a 'protest'. 'They
don't want you to do this' is the message. 'Take back control!'

One way to use reactance is to set up a situation where the
reader 'rebels' by buying into your message:

You might not believe this, but *WireCo* broadband
could be five times faster than your current service.

By suggesting that the reader might not believe the benefit,
this 'challenges' them to do just that.

Or you could try a more passive, softly-softly approach:

The benefits of switching to *EnergyCo* are crystal
clear. But of course, the final decision is yours.

This is like an inverted call to action: giving the reader
permission *not* to act. But because the benefits are 'crystal
clear', that obviously wouldn't be the smart play.

Embedded commands

In chapter 6, we saw the power of commands. Embedded commands are a neuro-linguistic programming (NLP) technique to use that power in a less obvious way.[72]

An embedded command is a sentence within a sentence, usually formed as an imperative. For example:

> You can <u>visit our showroom</u> any time between 9am and 5pm.

As we saw in chapter 11, the mind tends to latch on to concrete images and disregard the rest. Here, the concrete image in the sentence is the command 'visit our showroom'. Even though it's placed in a setting that's much more permissive ('can', 'any time'), NLP suggests that the reader's main takeaway will be the action you want them to take.

Not everyone accepts the theories of NLP, but this is a technique that you can easily throw in for a potential gain without harming the rest of your copy.

The double bind

A double bind looks like a choice between two alternatives, but in reality both paths lead to the same place. For example:

> You can order online or drop into our store to browse and buy a selection of our sofas.

The reader has two choices, but both entail a purchase. The idea is to present alternatives at one level (how to purchase) that amount to the same thing at a higher level (make a purchase). In this case, both alternatives are also embedded commands ('order online' and 'drop into our store').

---

72 *Teach yourself NLP* by Steve Bavister and Amanda Vickers, Hodder Education, 2004, p. 195.

Distinction bias

Distinction bias is the tendency to choose an option that seems different from alternatives that are presented at the same time. Even though we might be happy with a particular option on its own, we might see it differently when it's compared with other things.

In copywriting, this means moving the conversation from the benefits of one product to the contrasts between multiple products. Focus on how the product is different from competitors or alternatives, choosing a frame of comparison that favours the product. For example:

> While most controllers only have three ways to programme your heating, *ToastyHome* has five.

Readers should *really* be asking themselves how many programming methods are enough, or whether they even care. But if you frame their decision as a choice between two alternatives, one of which seems worse, they'll tend to choose the 'better' one.

TRY THIS

Psych 'em out

See if you can verbally influence someone using one of the techniques in this chapter. Nothing heavy – do it with something that's not that important, like deciding where to go for lunch.

15

HIT THE RIGHT **TONE**

Create a tone of voice to convey a consistent
character across everything you write for a brand.

What is tone of voice?

Our personalities show most clearly in the words we choose.
And it's exactly the same for brands.

Tone of voice is the personality of a brand, reflected in
its words. Just as you might recognise the sound of your
favourite band, or the style of your favourite painter, so you
can recognise some brands by the way they write or speak.

Tone of voice helps brands connect with readers by
communicating *consistency*, *character* and *value*. These three
levels support each other as shown in the diagram overleaf.
Let's look at each one in more detail.

Consistency

See what you think of this copy:

> Thanks a bunch for buying the *Toast-o-Matic*! You're
> totes gonna love her – she'll be your BFF beside the
> breadbin for years to come!

> To utilise the *Toast-o-Matic*, insert one or two slices of bread into the device and depress the activation lever. Note that the lever should never be subjected to excessive force.
>
> When the timer runs out, your toast will pop up automatically. If you want to get it out before then, press the red cancel button.

The problem here isn't the literal meaning. It's pretty clear what the product is, and how to use it. But the tone of voice is all over the place.

The first paragraph is upbeat and chirpy, almost manic. The second is stuffy and formal, and comes across as rather

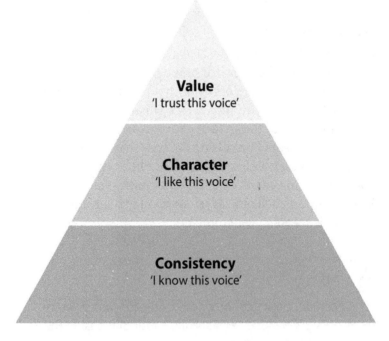

Value
'I trust this voice'

Character
'I like this voice'

Consistency
'I know this voice'

Three levels of communication with tone of voice, each supporting the one above

old-fashioned. And the third is somewhere between the two: informal and relaxed, but without much flavour of its own.

A brand's tone of voice needs to be *consistent* so that readers realise when the same 'person' is 'speaking'. Consistency paints a clear and stable picture in readers' minds of what a brand is like. Then, when the brand speaks, people think, 'I know this voice'. If the tone of voice isn't consistent, people can't remember it, or recognise it.

This consistency extends across different products, ads, campaigns and marketing channels, and also over time. Marketing comes and goes, but the brand's voice stays pretty much the same. That's what makes the difference between long-term strategic brand writing and tactical, project-by-project copywriting.

There's a parallel here with visual brand identity. Brands use consistent symbols, typography, colour and imagery to get the same 'look and feel' across everything they produce. If I say 'McDonald's', you can probably already see yellow and red, or a curvy 'M'. Tone of voice does the same thing with words.

To make this link clear, some marketers call tone of voice 'verbal identity'. It's a better name in a way, because it shows that words are just as important as visuals, and that they shape what a brand actually *is*, not just the way it talks. But I'm sticking with 'tone of voice' here because it's more widely used.

Some brands make their tone of voice consistent across *everything* they write, right through to the signs in the car park or the scripts used by call-centre staff. That sort of commitment can be a major business project that goes far beyond the job of the copywriter, or indeed the whole marketing team. It's very hard work, but it sends a powerful message to everyone who encounters the brand: we speak with one voice.

Character

A brand that people remember but don't particularly like is just mental clutter. But once your tone of voice is consistent, you can use it to express a unique personality that readers like. In other words, consistency can be the foundation for *character*.

We've seen how the most effective copy uses creative ideas and engaging writing to make products more distinctive and appealing. Tone of voice does the same thing at a higher level, so that everything a brand says engages readers in the same distinctive way. So as well as thinking 'I know this voice', readers also think 'I like this voice', or 'This voice speaks to me'.

When people like a brand's character, they're more receptive to its marketing messages. They may even look forward to them, or deliberately seek them out, as UK consumers do with John Lewis's Christmas TV ads.

This feeling of attraction can be another intangible benefit of choosing a brand. The brands we like say the things we want to hear, or the things we'd like to say. We give them our attention, or even our love, and they reward us by making all the right noises, like a cat purring when we stroke it.

Just as not everyone will like a film or a song, so not everyone will like a brand. So making a brand likeable doesn't mean trying to be universally popular. It means identifying a target audience – like we did in chapter 4 – and making the brand's voice appeal to them.

Value

A brand that people like is great, but it's still just entertainment. There's one more step to the top of the pyramid.

As we saw in chapter 13, consistency and liking can be very persuasive. That's why brands that succeed in making themselves consistently likeable can also communicate *value*. That takes readers from 'I know this voice' and 'I like this voice' to 'I trust this voice'. A brand that people see as valuable and trustworthy has deep and long-lasting selling power.

The first brands were simple signs. When British brewer Bass put a red triangle on its casks of pale ale in 1855, it was telling beer drinkers that they could expect a certain taste whenever they saw it. Even customers who couldn't read got the message.

Over the years, brands have taken on much more complex and subtle meanings, because 'good quality' is no longer enough to stand out. But the basic idea is the same: a brand is a promise of a certain type of value. Tone of voice makes sure that promise always comes across the same way, no matter what the product, time or situation.

A logo or a slogan isn't a brand, any more than a house is a home. Brands are what people think of them, and it's these perceptions that give them their commercial clout. When Apple brings out a new iPhone, it doesn't have to start promoting it from scratch, as if it was a start-up firm. The established power of its brand means that when Apple speaks, people listen.

To be clear, people's perceptions of a brand aren't produced by tone of voice alone. Actual product experiences are far more powerful, and the many other aspects of marketing and promotion are important too. But the right tone can still encourage people to try a brand, or stay loyal to it, by putting brand experiences into words.

Exploring brand character

Just as the things we say reflect our own personalities, so the words that brands use reflect theirs. So before you can create a tone of voice, you need to know the character of the brand.

Start by imagining the brand as a person. Now, ask yourself:

- What are they like?
- What's important to them?
- How do they go about their work?
- Who are their friends?
- What clothes do they wear?
- What car do they drive?
- Where do they live? What's their house like?
- What are their interests and hobbies?
- What's their favourite food, film, book, music?

These are just suggestions. You can use whatever themes you like, however trivial, as long as they tell you something useful. So your brand prefers Digestives to Custard Creams? No problem. Sometimes, those little details say a lot about someone's character.

Use your answers to write a character summary for the brand. Here's an example for a fictitious maker of premium handmade garden tools:

Who are *Greenleaf Garden Tools*?

We love gardening, even boring jobs like weeding and clearing leaves, and we want other people to love it too. Whatever the weather, we'd rather be outside, preferably with our hands in the earth. Gardening feeds our soul.

We like cosy woollen jumpers, listening to *The Archers* and a nice big mug of tea – all enjoyed in the garden, of course.

We think a job worth doing is worth doing properly, and we know that it's best to do it with really nice, well-made tools.

We're honest and dependable, like a friend you can always turn to when things get rough. We value things that last, not fads and fashions.

Greenleaf
Garden Tools

Greenleaf's visual identity

Be human

You're aiming to give the brand a human voice. So when you're exploring its character, make sure you focus on human traits, not marketing terms or corporate buzzwords.

The problem with that sort of business-speak is that it doesn't help you stand out. For example, lots of firms say they're 'innovative', or that they 'provide solutions'. Others claim to be 'passionate' about what they do. Those things may well be true, in their way. But if everyone else is saying them too, they won't lead to a distinctive tone.

As we saw in chapter 11 ('Be specific'), the antidote to abstraction is detail. Get down to grassroots by digging into the *how* and the *what*. How do you innovate, exactly? What makes you feel passionate? What are your solutions, and what problems do they solve? How do they help?

For example, an 'innovative' cleaning-products company might say 'We like making nasty jobs nicer', or 'We want people to be amazed at how clean their homes are'. Those sentiments get much closer to the people and ambitions behind the innovation. And they point the way forward to distinctive values like 'helpful', 'amazement' and 'delight'.

The best way to get into these human traits is to talk to humans. Sometimes, the character of young or small companies is very close to that of the founder(s), so you can easily get a sense of it simply by talking to them. In larger firms, character is less person-specific, but still real. It's there in the style of the team meeting, the atmosphere of the canteen, the décor of the office, the clothes people wear.

Spend some time at a company and you'll soon get a sense of 'how we do things around here'.

Be honest

Tone of voice isn't fiction. It needs to reflect the experience readers will actually have when they buy and use a product, or work with a company. Otherwise it simply won't ring true, and it will be impossible for the people using the tone to keep up the pretence.

Sometimes, firms use tone to express their aspirations. Many want to be like Innocent Drinks, with its upbeat, quirky tone. But that tone reflects the character of Innocent's founders and the brand they spent many years developing. So while it certainly has things to teach other brands, the Innocent tone isn't a coat that they can put on at will.

Brand guru BJ Cunningham tells the story of his consulting work for insurance firm Pinnacle. Like many financial services firms these days, they wanted a softer tone for their branding. But internally, employees called the firm 'cynical

The Innocent tone of voice: often imitated,
rarely equalled – and not for everybody

Pinnacle' because of its reluctance to pay out on claims. BJ told them this was a strength, not a weakness. Who wants to buy insurance from a soft 'n' cuddly firm that pays every claim and then has to charge big premiums as a result?[73]

The lesson is that there's always a good side to 'bad' characteristics. You're not cynical; you're rigorous. You're not boring; you're dependable. You're not old; you're well established. You're not unoriginal; you're good at finding improvements.

People choose a brand because of what it is, not what it pretends to be. Honesty is the best policy; firms should own their character and use it as a foundation for their tone.

From character to values

The next step is to boil down your brand character into brand values.

Brand values are simple statements of essential truth about a brand. They sum up why a brand exists, what it stands for and how it helps its customers. They're the character traits that should shine through in all its communications.

Some brands have a very clear sense of their values, and may already have captured them in a brand identity document. Others may have a vague idea, but without writing anything down. And some will never have considered them at all. Wherever the brand is now, you need to get a clear picture of its values before you can develop a tone of voice.

Let's go back to *Greenleaf Garden Tools*. They might describe their values something like this:

Outdoorsy	Love gardening	Down to earth
Appreciate quality	Hard-working	Hearty
Committed	Craft	Homely
Good with hands	Diligent	Dependable

---

73 BJ was the creator of Death cigarettes, a radical experiment in honest branding. Read his profile at tinyurl.com/bjprofile

This sort of brain-dump is a great start, but it needs sharpening up.

Some of these values, like 'committed', are fairly generic. They may be true, but anybody could say them, so they won't help the brand stand out. We can put them to one side.

Others, like 'appreciate quality', are hygiene factors. They mean a lot to the *Greenleaf* team, but they're not really plus points for customers. Nobody wants poor quality; 'good quality' is just the least you would expect. So we can discard these values too.

Other values are near-duplicates, like 'outdoorsy' and 'love gardening', or 'down to earth' and 'homely'. They're not really distinct, just different views of the same thing. We can probably roll them into one.

Overall, we could boil down *Greenleaf*'s values to just four: *gardening, dependable, homely* and *craft*. Here's how the brand might sum those up:

Love gardening	**Depend on us**
Gardening feeds our soul. Any job, any time of year, we just want to be out there with our hands in the earth. And we want others to feel the same way.	Rain or shine, we're always here, like a friend you can turn to when times get rough – or like a garden that's always waiting for you.
Home and dry	**Craft people**
We love the feeling of being at home, among family, where everything is OK.	We love working with our hands, and making fine tools that make hard work a little easier.

You don't need loads of values to define a brand. The more you have, the more you risk repeating or contradicting yourself. Three to five values are enough to define a unique location within the universe of writing styles.

By this point, your values should be in a state where you'd be happy to publish them, or use them in marketing. Whether you do so depends on what the values are. For example, if one of your values is 'modesty' or 'understatement', then banging on about it in public might not be consistent. Values come through in what you *don't* say too.

From values to tone

Having found the brand's values, you need to work out how they will translate into tone. That means using your values as a base to describe how the brand will express itself in writing.

The table below shows some characteristics you might also want to think about. It's not a quiz; you only need to consider the ones that are relevant.

I've presented them as choices between two opposites. In reality, they're more like points on a scale, or locations in a landscape. For example, your brand might be a bit quirky without going the full *Mighty Boosh*, or use a few literary flourishes without sounding like *Wuthering Heights*.

Is the brand...	...or is it
Serious	Silly
Casual	Formal
Respectful	Irreverent
Earnest	Cynical
Optimistic	Downbeat
Warm	Detached
Hipster	Fogeyish
Radical	Traditional
Practical	Romantic
Vulgar	Refined
Down to earth	Head in the clouds
Effervescent	Laid-back
Authoritative	Rebellious

Is the brand...	...or is it
Strident	Reticent
Forthright	Coy
Commanding	Cajoling
Wholesome	Decadent
Conversational	Literary

Throughout this book, I've tried to use the simplest words I can. But when it comes to describing tone of voice, you sometimes need more unusual words to pinpoint exactly what you mean. There's no point saying 'bluey green' or 'greeny blue' when the word you really need is 'turquoise'. For example, you could say the *Economist* ads in chapter 9 were 'funny', 'cynical' or 'clever'. But in my view, the *one word* that describes them is 'sardonic'. Distinctive character depends on distinctive words.

You might also want to go back to the brand character you thought about earlier, and use those human characteristics to describe the tone, as if the brand was a person. For example:

Age	How old is the brand?
	Is it a child, a teenager, a young adult, middle-aged, senior?
Gender	Is the brand feminine, masculine, neither or both at once?
Homeland	Does the brand come from a particular country or region?
	Is English its first language?[74]
Time period	Does the brand come from a certain time and place – Victorian England, 1960s Carnaby Street, 1970s Los Angeles?

---

74 See the Hyposwiss ads in chapter 9 for an example of a brand deliberately sounding 'foreign'.

References to culture, or even other brands, may help you describe your tone in broad terms. For example, *Greenleaf Garden Tools* could describe its tone very roughly as '*Gardeners' Question Time* meets M&S'. It may not be enough guidance to start writing, but it puts you in the right ballpark.

Some choices in these areas could make it much harder to write for the brand. For example, if you're British, you've probably heard and read a fair amount of American English. But actually writing it well enough to convince a native speaker is a different matter. All it takes is one 'pavement' instead of 'sidewalk' and you've outed yourself as a limey.

A similar point applies to readers: using a subtle, complex or allusive tone might mean sacrificing some accessibility. For example, if you were writing for a French brand in English, you might feel that dropping in some French phrases would give your writing a certain *je ne sais quoi*. But if readers don't understand them, it could be a *faux pas*.

You might also decide to go against some of the general advice in earlier chapters of this book – not randomly, but in a conscious, deliberate way. For example, if you want a flowery, ornate style, it probably won't be simple, punchy and light on description (all covered in chapter 12). And if your brand is very artistic or literary, it might not use conversational language (chapter 11).

As you make these choices, ask yourself whether the extra impact of a distinctive style is worth the trade-off in terms of accessibility. You're looking for a balance between style and substance, so readers get the message *and* appreciate the way it's delivered.

As well as describing the tone, you might want to set some technical guidelines on how to write it. For example:

Length	Are there any guidelines on the length of headings, sentences, paragraphs and so on?
Formatting	Will the brand use or avoid any particular text formats? (Bullet points, subheadings, etc)
Pace and flow	How quickly will the brand talk? Will it sound loose and languid, or clipped and concise?
Grammar	Will the brand obey all rules of grammar, or will it bend them from time to time? Are there any grammatical forms (such as the passive voice) that the brand will try to avoid?
Description	How will the brand describe things? How many adjectives and adverbs will it use?
Referring to self and others	Will the brand call itself 'we', and the reader 'you'? (This is usually the best approach – see chapter 11)
Conversational language	Will the brand use slang or made-up words? Will the brand use contractions like 'we're', 'you'll' and so on?
Preferred terms and domain language	Are there any words or phrases that should always be used? (For example, referring to service users as 'clients', or referring to particular religions or ethnic origins in a certain way) Are there any words and phrases specific to the sector that should be used?
Reserved words	Are there any words or phrases that can only be used in certain ways? (For example, 'advice' has a specific legal meaning in financial services)
Forbidden words	Are there any words and phrases that the brand will avoid completely? (For example: gendered language; describing people with an illness as 'sufferers')
Other standards	Will the brand use any third-party standards, such as the Chicago Manual of Style,[75] Harvard reference style[76] or *Hart's Rules*?[77]

75 See chicagomanualofstyle.org
76 See the Wikipedia article at tinyurl.com/harvardrefs
77 *New Hart's Rules: The Oxford Style Guide*, OUP, 2014.

Here's how *Greenleaf Garden Tools* might describe its tone, using its values as a structure:

> Our tone of voice is warm, practical and down to earth.
>
> Our roots are in the English countryside, but we love all types of garden, wherever they are.
>
> Our voice sounds like an enthusiastic gardener, probably in her 30s or 40s, showing you round her garden and sharing her ideas and experiences.

Value	How it comes through in our writing
Love gardening	We talk about the experience of being outdoors: the seasons; the weather; the sights, colours, sounds and scents.
	We describe gardening jobs with positive language whenever we can ('keep flowerbeds clear' instead of 'get rid of weeds') and with a positive, can-do attitude.
	We don't talk down. We write in an inclusive way, so owners of smaller, urban or container gardens can still relate to what we say, and get value from it.
Depend on us	We describe what tools do with the general formula 'A does B, which helps you C'.
	We use simple, concrete 'doing' words wherever we can (like 'dig', 'plant', 'cut' and so on).
	Whenever we can, we avoid obscure gardening terms, especially abstract nouns (like 'scarification', 'propagation' and so on). If we have to use words like that, we explain what they mean.
Home and dry	We talk about the emotions of home: comfort, security, safety, familiarity, warmth, belonging, togetherness.
	We use relaxed 'weekend' words, not uptight 'working week' words. We use contractions (like 'don't', 'we'll' and so on) to express relaxation.

Craft people	We prize manual work and making things by hand, so we talk about the materials and processes that go into our tools with enthusiasm and respect.
	When we can, we link our craft in toolmaking with our customers' craft at gardening.

Vary the tone

So, if tone of voice has to be consistent, does that mean everything you write for a brand should sound exactly the same?

Whenever a brand speaks, it should always sound like the same person is talking. But we don't talk the same way all the time in real life. Our *personality* stays the same, but we adapt our tone to the situation we're in, the person we're talking to and, sometimes, what we're feeling ourselves.

Imagine you have an appointment with your bank to talk about a loan. The advisor greets you warmly when you arrive. As she explains your options, her manner becomes more teacher-like, making sure you understand. And when she goes over the terms and conditions, she might be serious, almost stern, warning you about what will happen if you miss your payments. Then she wraps up the meeting with the warm tone again. Throughout the meeting, she has been professional, authoritative and friendly – but those traits have come out in different ways depending on the context.

The same principle applies to brands. Tone of voice needs to flex to different situations by bringing different values to the fore at different times. Rules on tone should never prevent you from talking to readers in the right way for the job you need to do.

Let's go back to *Greenleaf Garden Tools*. A full-colour printed advert in the weekend press might shout out 'Love gardening' and 'Home and dry', with appealing imagery of a family garden. But a letter responding to a customer's complaint would dial those values right back and bring

'Depend on us' to the fore instead, expressing humility and the wish to make things right. Making everything *Greenleaf* wrote sound exactly the same would make for some pretty boring ads – or some truly infuriating letters.

In the end, it comes back to empathy (chapter 4). How would *you* like to receive this news, or be given this instruction? Think about that as well as the tone you want to achieve, and you'll soon find the right way forward.

Tone of voice guidelines

Once tone of voice is decided, it's usually recorded in a document containing guidelines on how to write for the brand. These guidelines crystallise tone of voice into something that can be worked on, shared and talked about. They also help everyone who writes for a brand to maintain a consistent tone in multiple projects over time. Tone guidelines are often integrated into broader brand documents that also cover brand values and visual identity.

A client might give you their tone of voice document to guide your copywriting. Assuming it's clear and coherent, it will give you a head-start in working out how your copy should sound.

Others clients might not have a written tone of voice, or may never have considered it at all. That's OK. You can still do a good job within the brief, and if the client likes their previous copy, you could strike a similar tone with yours.

Sometimes, tone of voice just grows out of writing. As you work on more and more copy projects for the same brand, you start to get a sense of how it should sound. The brand starts to 'sound more like itself'. You may never write down the rules you're following, or even think about them consciously. But you're still following them.

You may also need to write tone guidelines for a brand. How much you write depends on the purpose of the guidelines. If you're just making notes for your own use, they might be very brief. If you're writing a manual for a major brand that will be used by many different people, the guidelines might run to many pages. You might even be asked to offer guidance and training for the people who will write for the brand.

Your document could include:

- What the guidelines cover and who they're for
- A description of the brand and its character
- The brand's values and the reasons behind them
- High-level description of the tone of voice
- More detailed technical guidance on how to write in the tone of voice
- How the tone of voice should vary between different media, publications, channels or situations
- Dos and don'ts
- Examples, perhaps with explanatory notes

Five real-world tones of voice

Let's look at five tones of voice used by real brands and what makes them distinctive.

FreeAgent, the online accounting platform, has a tone that's authoritative but friendly and empathetic, with a bold sense of humour that sets it apart from rivals. Here's a popup from its website:

Self-assessment filing for 2016/17 is live

You can now file your 2016/17 Self Assessment return to HMRC well ahead of the January 31st deadline.

You may be tempted to put it off for now, but getting your return out of the way will mean avoiding that lurching feeling of guilt and existential despair that usually sets in around January.

The reference to people's aversion to sorting out their tax gets a wry smile of recognition, while the unexpectedly emotive language makes the message more memorable and humanises the brand. However, it's still clear that this is a message the reader should take seriously, and that the brand takes it seriously too.

Macmillan, the cancer support charity, have a very detailed tone of voice document that you can find online.[78] They sum up their writing instructions as 'PISA' – Personal, Inspiring, Straightforward, Active. They also recommend talking about 'people with cancer' rather than labelling them as 'patients'. Here's the opening of their 'About us' page:

> At Macmillan, we know how a cancer diagnosis can affect everything. So we're here to support you and help you take back some control in your life. From help with money worries and advice about work, to someone who'll listen if you just want to talk, we're here.

Too many corporate 'About us' pages sound like a boring old uncle reciting from his memoirs. Macmillan's is completely reader-focused – even on a page about them, there's still as much 'you' as 'we'. In line with PISA, the simple, active verbs like 'know', 'help' and 'listen' set out Macmillan's mission without falling into corporate or third-sector jargon (see 'Be active' in chapter 11).

Patek Philippe, the luxury watch brand, appeals to a very different mindset, and its tone of voice is very different too. It's formal, elevated and self-assured:

> The unparalleled renown and prestige that Patek Philippe has acquired amongst connoisseurs is not due solely to the perfection of the watches and the resources of knowledge and skill contained in the workshops.

78 At the time of writing, you can download it from tinyurl.com/macmillantone

> This undisputed supremacy also stems from the consistency with which the company has applied its philosophy of excellence ever since it was founded in 1839.
>
> That spirit is embodied in ten values that have always represented the very essence of Patek Philippe and will continue to do so for generations to come.

The meandering, intricate style conveys a sense of attention to detail that's entirely appropriate for a watchmaker. The noun-heavy sentence structures also give a 'translated' feel that emphasises the Swiss-ness of the brand. It's clear that heritage and continuity are important values – not just for Patek Philippe, but for its customers too.

The tone of Brewdog, the craft brewer, is energetic, confident and 'in your face'. Taking its cue from the firm's founders, it sounds like a young but highly skilled enthusiast who strongly believes in what they do. Here's the web copy for the 'Amplified' (read: very strong) range:

> Looking to turn it up to 11? We like your style. Our high-octane Amplified beers play host to some of the finest, most carefully constructed recipes known to man or dog.
>
> Looking for a beer with more bitterness than a human palate (or nipple) can detect? You're in the right place. Want to indulge that sweet tooth with a heather-infused chocolatey, roasty, decadently complex scotch ale? It's here.
>
> Elvis Juice, Jack Hammer, Hardcore IPA and Cocoa Psycho are our family of unbelievably intense, flavoursome, seductive and powerful beers. This is beermaking writ large.

Visit our bars or online shop to find out more. Take
your time. Sip. Enjoy.

Some product descriptions just, well, describe the product.
Brewdog's copy addresses the reader directly with questions
and commands, and throws in plenty of adjectives to evoke
the drinking experience (see 'Talk to your reader' and
'Make it real' in chapter 11). There's also a strong sense of
commitment and belief in Brewdog's own brewing expertise.

Finally, snack-maker Golden Wonder's tone is cheerful,
bouncy and casual. This on-pack copy uses conversational
language (chapter 11) with alliteration and rhyme (see 'Make
it rhyme', chapter 12) to put forward quality and flavour as
USPs (chapter 3). They even use exclamation marks:

> At Golden Wonder, our crisps are fully
> flavoured, from the way we cook them to our
> tongue-tingling seasonings!

> We only use the very finest spuds, peeled
> and cooked in sunflower oil until they're wonder-
> fully golden.

> Then comes the really tasty bit. We load every bag
> with our mouth-watering Cheese & Onion oomph,
> making sure each crisp has more punch per crunch!

In their very different ways, all these tones of voice achieve
the three aims we saw at the start of this chapter. They're
consistent, so each brand has a recognisable way of speaking.
Each has its own distinctive *character*, based in brand values
and designed to appeal to its target readers. And each one
uses tone to express different types of *value* that the brand
offers – from beating cancer to brewing beer.[79]

79 For a detailed guide to creating and using a tone of voice, see *Brand Language: Tone of Voice the Wordtree Way* by Liz Doig, Wordtree & Me Ltd, 2014.

TRY THIS

Values and tone

Choose a brand you know well – your favourite drink, magazine or clothing brand. What might its values be?

Now look at something written by the brand. It can be something as short as a product label or a tweet. How do its values come through in its copy?

16

DEALING WITH **FEEDBACK**

Make your client happy and keep your copy snappy.

About feedback

Dealing with client feedback is a big part of being a copywriter. You may feel your copy has hit the target, but before it can be used, your client has to agree. That means understanding and responding to their feedback without losing sight of the aims we've looked at so far.

Get your head right

There are two sides to dealing with feedback. There's the practical side, which involves amending your copy to satisfy your client while still meeting the brief. But there's also an emotional side, which is about hearing direct comments on your work without getting uptight or upset. And that can be a challenge if you've put a lot of work into your copy, or if you feel your ideas are really strong and deserve to be used as they are.

So it's important to remember that *the feedback is on the work, not you*. You may have put your heart and soul into your copy, but for now, you need to get some distance from it. You and your client are on the same side of the desk, working together to tackle the problem and improve the copy. Once your work is approved, you can identify with it more closely again.

Respect the feedback

In chapter 11, we talked about seeing things from the reader's side. When dealing with feedback, you need to take the same approach, but with the client.

Feedback can sometimes be frustrating, or even perplexing. But if you want to move forward, you need to meet the client where they are, and that means listening carefully to what they say and understanding the reasons behind it.

Remember: your client is doing the best they can with the resources they have. They want the project to succeed, just like you do, and they don't gain anything by messing you about for no reason.

It might be that your client hasn't worked with a copywriter that much, so they're unsure how to express their feedback. If so, it's your job as the senior partner to take up the slack and make this creative relationship work.

Read what's written

Feedback is hard to predict. You can produce copy that you feel is great, but your client asks for major changes. Or, despite doing your best, you might end up with something you feel is so-so – but the client loves it.

Therefore, any time and energy you spend trying to anticipate or second-guess feedback is probably wasted. Once your draft goes in, occupy yourself with another project in the meantime, or just get out of the office altogether. Also, try not to interpret silence as disapproval. It usually just means the client is busy with other things.

When the feedback arrives, give yourself time and space to process it. Even if you feel angry, don't fire off a defensive email straight away. Before you do anything, read the feedback slowly and carefully, so you fully understand what the client is saying and you don't start wrestling with what you *think* they've said, or what you expected them to say. Then, once you've properly understood the feedback, you can move on to dealing with it.

Negativity bias means that we give far more weight to negative feedback than positive. If you've ever obsessed over a little remark about your hair or clothes, even though you got loads of compliments on the same day, you'll know what I mean. So make a conscious effort to acknowledge the positive things the client is saying. If they say something like 'It's mostly great, but we just need a few tweaks,' believe them.

You are not the reader... and neither is your client

Copywriting projects can easily go off the rails at the feedback stage if everybody focuses so closely on the copy that they forget all about the reader.

As we saw in chapter 11 ('Don't write for the client') and chapter 12 ('Kill your darlings'), you're not the target audience for your copy, and neither is your client.

Just as you shouldn't put forward copy just because you like it, so your client shouldn't approve it just because *they* do. Instead, you should both agree that the copy meets the brief and will appeal to the reader. It may even be that *neither* of you particularly like it, but still you both agree that it's right for the project.

The same test should apply to feedback. If you're resisting a client's change, take a minute to ask yourself: 'Do I want to keep this copy because I believe it will work, or just because I like it?'

On the flip side, your client shouldn't reject something simply because they don't like it. You should really ask them to justify their changes in terms of the reader and the brief, rather than their own tastes. Obviously, that could get a bit awkward, and they might just overrule you in the end. But in the long run, you don't help your client by allowing them to tailor their marketing to themselves.

Wrong directions, wrong destination

Your copy can only be as good as the brief you were given. Before you dive into making changes, check the feedback against the brief. If the changes are so radical that acting on them would take the project in a completely new direction, one of two things has happened: either the brief was wrong in the first place, or new insights have emerged during the project that mean the brief needs to change.

That's not the end of the world, as long as you revise the brief now and confirm that the client is definitely happy with the new direction. Don't try to revise the brief implicitly, by just patching up the copy and hoping it will fly. Have the conversation with your client first.

Ask for examples

Sometimes, clients find it hard to express what they want, even with reference to the brief. So they fall back on saying 'I'll know it when I see it'. But if you go down that road, you'll end up submitting draft after draft until you stumble on the right answer – if you ever find it at all, that is.

Instead, ask the client to provide you with examples of the sort of thing they mean. After all, if they can recognise what works in your copy, they should be able to recognise it in someone else's, and save a lot of time and effort in the process.

When you see the examples, make sure you ask the client exactly what they like about them. It may not be what you expect. And if the examples seem to be incompatible with each other, you may need to go back and discuss the brief again. Or you may need to explain (respectfully) that one piece of copy can't do everything, or appeal to everybody.

Accept or reject the feedback

Accepting feedback can be hard when you've put a lot of time and effort into a draft. But if the client's changes are in line with the brief, and will improve the copy – or at least, not make it worse – you have to accept them.

At other times, you may consider the feedback very carefully, but decide that you really shouldn't act on it. Here are some reasons why you might do that:

- **It's technically wrong.** If the client's change would introduce a mistake in spelling, grammar or word usage, and there's no good reason for it, you should reject it. You'll usually be able to find an authoritative online resource to back you up.
- **It's against the brief**. As we've seen, if the change goes against the brief, you either need to reject the change or reconsider the brief itself.
- **It harms the copy**. The change might be in line with the brief, but still damage the copy in some other way. For example, it might mix up a metaphor (chapter 9), disrupt rhythm (chapter 12) or undermine a persuasive or psychological tactic (chapters 13 and 14). If the client doesn't write much for their own brand, it might be out of line with their own tone of voice (chapter 15). If so, you need to explain to them – carefully and tactfully – why the copy won't work as well if you make their change.
- **It's too much**. Once you've read a piece of copy a few times, it's easy to take what it does for granted, and decide that it needs to do more. A client thinking along these lines might ask you to cover more features or benefits, add more detail to the argument or appeal to more readers. But while they may be hoping to strengthen the copy, they'll probably end up watering it down. You'll need to help them see the copy through the eyes of a first-time reader, and point out the power of a clear, simple message.

If you do decide to reject the client's feedback, make sure you explain your reasoning to them. If they still disagree with you, you have to decide whether to push back or just give in. Your client isn't paying you to argue with them, but at the same time they're not paying you for bad advice. Some copywriters will die on a hill for a misplaced comma, while others can chill as long as the big picture looks OK. It's your call.

Work through the feedback

Once you've established what feedback you're going to act on, start working through the edits. If the client has provided a list of changes, print it out and tick them off as you go. If there are tracked changes in Word, you can address them one by one. This will give you a good feeling of making progress.

Comments added to a Word document are a good way to explain your thinking to the client right there as they read. You can do this even in your very first draft, but it's also a good idea to reply to the client's own comments or explain how you've decided to act (or not act) on the feedback. Notes in the accompanying email are OK, but they can easily get separated from the copy – for example, if it's circulated among a few different people.

Don't just work on a single version of your copy. At the very least, it's good practice to keep each version you send to the client, so you can track how it's changed over time and how you responded to feedback. If you're working on a single shared document on Google Drive or Dropbox, you may want to save offline backups for your own reference.

If you need to experiment, save a separate version as a 'sandbox' and work on that. If it turns out to be the way forward, great. If it's a dead end, you can retrace your steps without losing anything. Alternatively, if you need to make big cuts, make a 'trash' document and paste the bits you delete in there, so you can bring them back later on if you need to.

17

PROJECT TIPS

Hints and tips for different types of copywriting projects.

About this chapter

Here you'll find tips and suggestions for the main types of copywriting project you're likely to work on. While some are dos and don'ts, most are intended as suggestions for things to consider. Every brand and product is different, so use these tips to help you make the right choices, rather than following them to the letter.

Web pages[80]

- Make sure each page has a distinct theme or purpose. Split pages that are trying to do too much, combine pages that seem to duplicate each other and delete pages that have no real purpose.
- Write an informative headline (see chapter 6) that explains the purpose of the page for the benefit of both readers and search engines.
- For B2B service sites in particular, make sure visitors arriving at the site understand what it's about. Bear in

---

80 For more on writing for the web, see *How to Write Seductive Web Copy* by Henneke Duistermaat, Enchanting Marketing Ltd, 2013.

mind that any page can be a landing page – that is, visitors can use Google to arrive at any page within the site, not just the home page.

- Even if people do arrive at the home page, they're still unlikely to read all the pages of the site in order. Each page should work on its own as far as possible; *some* duplication across pages may be OK if it helps you achieve this goal.
- Within pages, people will probably skim-read or scroll around, so use subheadings and short sections to break up the copy. Make your subheadings descriptive as well as persuasive, and take great care when using intrigue headlines (see 'Create intrigue' in chapter 6).
- Don't just write a long page of text. Think about how you could break it up with subheadings, columns, bullets,

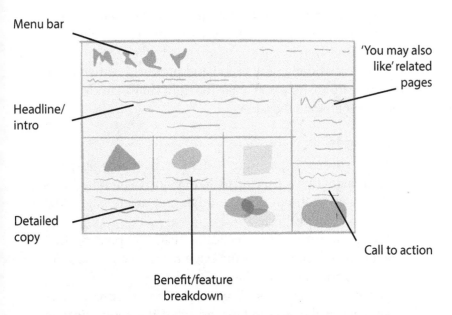

A 'wireframe', or rough layout for a web page. When writing your copy, use tables in Word to show how your copy could be laid out tables, pullout quotes and other visual devices (see 'Use visuals and formats' in chapter 7). This is particularly important for longer content such as case studies.

- Think about the layout. If you're not working to a wireframe (a rough outline design), use tables and text styles to create a basic version of the layout in your document so you can show others what you have in mind.

- If you're giving information, use a structure like the family tree (chapter 7) so skim-readers get the most important points first. The family tree structure can apply to sections within a page, or pages within a section of the site.

- Don't write too much. Think about how the page will look on phones and tablets. For many sites, one or two sentences per paragraph is fine. Consider using punchy text fragments ('Make it punchy' in chapter 12) if they are appropriate for the brand.

- Make pages long enough for the job they have to do, and the information the reader needs at that point. A home page introduces the brand and guides readers to wherever they want to go next. A product page tells the reader what they need to know about a product and persuades them to choose it. A case study or a how-to guide gives the reader plenty of detail, letting them go deeper and learn more.

- When describing products or services, see things from the reader's side, use concrete language and evoke the experience of using the product (all covered in chapter 11).

- For commercial sites, you'll probably want a call to action ('Get in touch', 'Book now', 'Shop the range', etc – see chapter 8) at the end of many pages. Since readers' experience of the site is open-ended, you might also want a call to action in a position that's always visible, like a top navigation or sidebar.

- For larger sites, consider adding subsidiary calls to action that lead to related pages. Think carefully about what the reader might want to do next, and where you could guide them within your site. You could add 'Now read...' links at the end of pages, or put them in a 'Related pages' or 'You may also like' panel in a sidebar.
- Use descriptive text for links – for example, 'Browse our range', 'Get in touch' and so on. This helps readers know what they're getting before they click, and is also good for SEO.

Audio and video scripts

These points apply to broadcast ads, introduction movies, explanatory videos and anything else where your copy will be spoken aloud rather than printed.

- Find out how long the finished media will be (30 seconds, two minutes or whatever) and work out how much to write. Normal speaking speed is about 150–180 words per minute, but different moods might call for different pacing (see 'Pace yourself' in chapter 12) and you may not need continuous speech throughout.
- Set out your copy in a table with two columns. The left one is for the words that will be spoken, and the right one is for whatever else will be happening (sound effects, on-screen events, graphics and so on).
- Write one sentence of copy in each row, indicating who will speak it (an on-screen narrator, a voiceover, a character), and indicate whatever visuals will accompany it alongside.
- Use familiar words and short sentences for maximum clarity (see 'Make it simple' in chapter 12). Remember, your 'reader' is a listener. They can't see the words you're writing and they can't go back if they miss something. They may only hear your message once, so they need to understand it first time.

- Your opening is crucial (see 'Start strong' in chapter 7). Think about ways you can offer a benefit (chapter 3), evoke a problem (chapter 7), talk about the listener's situation (chapter 4) or use a creative angle (chapter 9) to create interest right from the start.
- Think about how you could use storytelling (see 'Tell a story' in chapter 11). Reading a story is powerful, but watching or hearing one is even more so. What events or experiences relevant to the product could you make into a story? What other views on it could you explore (see 'Switch perspectives' in chapter 9)?
- For most projects, you'll want to match the listener's language so your script sounds like a conversation (see 'Use the same words the reader uses' in chapter 11). However, your script should also be in line with the brand's tone of voice (chapter 15), so that it sounds like the brand would speak.
- To make your script more engaging, address the listener directly as 'you' (see 'Talk to your reader' in chapter 11).
- Think about visuals and sound together. Your copy should work with whatever is happening on screen or on the soundtrack, so they come together to say one thing. At certain points, you may not need to describe, explain or comment on the action at all (see 'Use images' and 'Show, don't tell' in chapter 9).
- For longer information films, consider using on-screen captions or prompts to reinforce key points, or as 'subheadings' to indicate that a new section is starting. If you do, make sure the spoken and written words match up, so people aren't hearing one thing but reading another.
- If you're explaining complex ideas, consider how you could use visual techniques like animation to make them clearer. Even simple flowcharts, timelines or diagrams can help people get a grip of processes and relationships

much more easily (see 'Use visuals and formats' in chapter 7). If you're using a metaphor (chapter 9), you could show it as you describe it.

- Think about who else could speak, apart from a narrator. Could the characters in a story speak, or could the story be told completely through their dialogue? Could an expert speak, providing authority (chapter 13)? Could a customer speak, sharing their positive experience?
- Read your script out loud, or ask someone else to read it. Does it move forward at a consistent pace? Is the rhythm smooth and flowing? Could you make it more pleasing with alliteration, or even rhyme? (All covered in chapter 12.)
- Consider signing off with a tagline that sums up the whole message or value proposition, and/or a call to action (chapter 8) that tells the listener what to do now.

Sales letters

These points also apply to landing pages and any other self-contained pieces of longer copy that are designed to take visitors from first interest right through to a purchase or enquiry.[81]

- If you can, use the reader's first name in the salutation (for example, 'Dear Jenny'). Throughout the letter, address the reader as 'you' and refer to yourself as 'we' or 'I', to show that this is a personal communication.
- Spend time getting the headline right – it's the most important part of your letter (see chapter 6). If the headline doesn't work, whatever comes after it is irrelevant. Write several options for your headline, then choose the best. If you can't find the right headline, write the main part of the letter first (see 'Write the middle first' in chapter 7).

---

81 For a comprehensive guide to writing sales letters, see *How to Write Sales Letters that Sell* by Drayton Bird, Kogan Page, 2002.

- Aim for a headline that tells the reader you're talking to them, sets up a problem/solution (see 'Solve a problem' in chapter 7) and mentions the main benefit.
- Make your opening as vivid and engaging as you can (see 'Start strong' in chapter 7). Show you understand the reader's situation and feelings (chapter 4). Describe the problem from every angle, and explain exactly why it's a challenge for the reader. (If you're seeking support for a charity, talk about the problem faced by the people the charity wants to help.)
- Poke the problem. Talk about what will happen if the reader doesn't act, or if they keep doing what they're doing. You could appeal to the endowment effect or loss aversion (chapter 14) to point out what the reader will lose if they do nothing.
- Next, introduce the product as the solution to the problem. Explain its benefits (chapter 3), and how it addresses all the aspects of the problem you raised before. Talk about how it's helped other people (see 'Social proof' in chapter 13), with testimonials if possible. Bring in other voices to strengthen your case (see 'Take different views' in chapter 7).
- If necessary, establish your own credibility as someone who can speak about the product, perhaps with the principles of liking or authority (chapter 13).
- If you need to talk about the cost, put it in a different context (see 'Reframe costs' in chapter 14) to make it seem less significant. Explain how much value the product will provide for the price – savings, time saved, other purchases the reader doesn't have to make and so on. Express this value as an amount of money if you can, to show that a purchase is an investment that will offer a positive return.
- Address the reader's likely objections to ease their anxiety about buying, donating or responding (see 'Overcoming objections' in chapter 13). Think back to what the reader

wants and feels (see 'What does your reader want?' and 'How does your reader feel?' in chapter 4) and use it to make their desire stronger than their objection.

- Ask for the sale with the call to action (chapter 8). Tell the reader exactly what to do and show them that it won't be difficult or complicated (see 'Show that it's quick and easy' in chapter 8). Encourage them with extras, discounts, free trials and money-back offers if you can.
- Consider using a PS to restate the main benefit and the call to action.
- For longer letters, use subheads to break up the text. Use the same techniques that make main headlines compelling, such as creating intrigue, asking questions or explaining why (all covered in chapter 6).
- Use linking words and phrases like 'Actually', 'What's more', 'In fact' or 'That's why' to keep the reader moving from one paragraph to the next.
- Remember that readers tend to skim-read and latch on to things that stand out – headings, words in bold, bullet points, captions and PSs. Try and make these elements sell the benefits, as well as guiding the reader or giving them information.

Emails

These tips apply to any email where you're trying to get the reader to take action – make a purchase, visit a website, make contact and so on.

- Know your aim (chapter 4). Be absolutely clear on who the reader is and what you want them to do. The list you are targeting defines the reader's profile. Work out what they want, how you're offering to help them and what they need to do next, and use that to keep your copy on track.
- The subject line is crucial, because it determines whether your email will even be opened, let alone read. Treat it like a headline (chapter 6).

- Subject lines that refer to benefits (chapter 3), news (chapter 6), special offers (perhaps time-limited – see 'Scarcity' in chapter 13) or social proof (chapter 13) are likely to work well. Your aim is to make the reader want something they can only get by opening the email.
- Use intrigue (chapter 6) with care in subject lines. People generally want to know what an email's about before they read it, so straightforward description often works best. Focus on converting your most likely prospects (chapter 4) rather than trying to cast the net too wide.
- If you want to generate intrigue, you could start with 'How', 'How to', 'What' or 'Why', promising valuable knowledge, or tell a human-interest story, perhaps of someone who used the product (see 'Tell a story' in chapter 11).
- Colourful emojis in the subject line can make an email jump out of the screen, but may not be right for the brand's tone of voice (chapter 15). They work best when they're directly relevant to the product (not just eye-catching stars or smileys).
- If you can, use the reader's name in the salutation ('Dear Paul') and maybe in the subject line too.
- The best emails are from people we know and like. Talk to the reader one-to-one, using everyday words, as if you were writing to a friend or colleague (see 'Talk to your reader', 'Write like you talk' and 'Write for someone you know' in chapter 11). Use empathy to show you understand the reader – but with a light touch (see 'How does your reader feel?' in chapter 4).
- Put yourself in the reader's place and imagine receiving this email (see 'See it from the reader's side' in chapter 11). What value does it offer? What problem does it solve? Why would you be interested?
- Email is one place where short copy usually works better than long, so keep an eye on length. Readers are increasingly likely to be on mobile devices, where they

can see the subject line and the first few words of the body copy before they open, so it's even more important to get to the point.

- Don't waste the reader's time by telling them things they already know (see 'Give information' in chapter 7). If you're using the problem/solution approach (see 'Solve a problem' in chapter 7), state the problem as clearly and concisely as you can (one short paragraph, or one sentence), then get straight into product benefits.

- Aim for a tight, linear flow, with no detours. Take a direct path – for example: problem, solution, benefits, proof, call to action. As in sales letters (see above), use connecting phrases to draw the reader from one sentence to the next and keep them engaged.

- Use the design to your advantage (see 'Use visuals and formats' in chapter 7 and 'Use images' in chapter 9), but bear in mind that sometimes, plain text works just as well (and can be better at evading spam filters). A good plain-text email is the equivalent of a well-crafted letter.

- Include a single, clear, short call to action (chapter 8) and make sure it's highlighted in the design. Since it will almost certainly be a link, look at the landing page and make sure it will follow up on the email in a logical way, so the conversation with the reader continues smoothly. Minimise the number of clicks to a sale – for example, by linking directly to a product page rather than dumping the reader at the home page.

- A PS can be a good place to restate a key benefit and tie it to a point about scarcity (chapter 13). However, this may not be appropriate for every brand, or for every design.

- Use A/B testing to find out what works best. Platforms such as Mailchimp will automatically test different subject lines (and other elements) against each other.[82]

---

82   See tinyurl.com/mailchimpab

Display advertisements

These guidelines are for any advert that uses text and graphics in a fixed-size format – press advertisements, posters, online banner ads and so on.

- Before you start, make sure you've sorted out the brief (chapter 5). Space is limited, so you must know who you're writing for, what you're offering them and which benefit you are going to put centre stage.

- The more things you try to cover, the less impact your ad will have. Choose a main benefit and focus on that.

- Think about a creative angle (chapter 9) for your ad – a way to be different, emotive or witty. Remember, your creative idea should dramatise the main benefit while answering the brief and selling the product.

- Spend time on your headline (chapter 6) and try out different versions of it. It needs to express the main benefit, sum up the creative concept and/or intrigue the reader so they want to read on.

- Consider whether you can achieve your aim with the headline alone, perhaps with help from imagery. Think about what pictures could say that words can't, and vice versa. Draw a scamp, or rough sketch, to help you see how imagery, headline and body copy work together (see 'Use images' in chapter 9).

- If you're writing body copy, think about opening with the reader's situation or viewpoint before guiding them across the bridge to the things you want to say (see 'See it from the reader's side' in chapter 11).

- Give your body copy some shape by telling a story, taking different views, offering the solution to a problem or going step by step (see 'Tell a story' in chapter 11, and chapter 7 for the other techniques).

- Focus each sentence on a unique point and get rid of duplication (see 'Make it simple' in chapter 12).

- Your copy should be long enough to do its job, but no longer (see 'Get the length right' in chapter 12).
- Beware of becoming over-attached to ideas, images, phrases or plays on words that are actually getting in the way (see 'Kill your darlings' in chapter 12).
- Consider returning to the main theme or the creative concept at the end of your body copy, to give your copy a pleasing shape and round it off on a high note rather than just tailing off.
- Tell the reader what to do next (unless it's obvious) with a clear and simple call to action (chapter 8).

Print projects

These guidelines are for multi-page printed publications like leaflets, brochures, catalogues, guidebooks and so on.

- First, work out the target length for your copy, in words. Print projects are shaped by the balance between choice of format, printing costs and number of pages. Since print is often the biggest cost, the client will probably want to choose a format upfront – for example, an A5 16-page self-cover booklet – and let that guide the project. You can use this to work out how much you'll need to write.
- Alternatively, you can write whatever is necessary and see how many pages it makes, but this leaves a question mark over print costs until the text is approved. For most commercial projects, writing to fit is the best approach. (If your copy will be published in a digital format like a PDF, length may be less of an issue.)
- Don't forget to allow for graphics, photos and white space. If you can, talk to the designer to get a sense of how many words will appear on each page. If they've created a sample layout, refer to that.
- Consider what material will be needed as well as the main copy – an introduction, a contents page, an imprint, contact details, copyright notice, image credits, and so on.

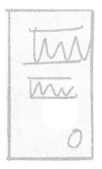

Front cover

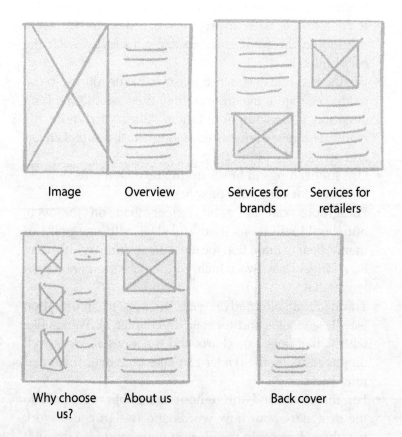

| Image | Overview | | Services for brands | Services for retailers |

| Why choose us? | About us | | | Back cover |

Planning out an eight-page booklet, spread by spread

Remember you may have the inside front, inside back and outside back cover to play with.

- Plan out your copy page by page, or spread by spread as shown in the diagram. (A spread is two pages side by side.) Most brochures and catalogues begin each new section on a new page. If you're working in spreads, always try to begin a section on a left-hand page.
- Think about a title for the whole publication, to appear on the front cover. It may need to be a simple description, but not always. The phrase that people involved use to refer to the project doesn't necessarily have to become the title.
- If your title is more expressive than descriptive, use a subtitle on the front cover to explain exactly what the publication is.
- For the inside pages, write informative headlines so the reader can find the information they need. Grabbing attention is less important here, since you know the reader is already interested enough to have picked up and opened the publication.
- Use subheadings to break up the text. Don't just write a big block for each page or spread.
- Paragraphs can be a bit longer than on the web, but should still be focused and deal with one point or theme. Bear in mind that the measure (column width) may be relatively narrow, which will make long paragraphs look 'taller'.
- Think about alternative ways to present information (see 'Use visuals and formats' in chapter 7). Things like tables, diagrams, flowcharts and timelines all work well on paper, when the reader can take time over them and refer back.
- For the cover and throughout the publication, talk to the designer about how words and design could work together. How could the ideas in your copy feed through into the layout?

- Unlike websites, printed materials can't be corrected after they appear. For longer projects particularly, consider asking a proofreader to check the text before it's printed (see 'Check it… or get it checked' in chapter 12).

Social media posts

These guidelines are for short texts to be published on social media platforms such as Twitter and Facebook.

- Always remember the reader's situation (see chapter 4). They didn't go online to seek out sponsored posts or company updates. They didn't ask for your message, and even if they did follow an account or like a page, they won't automatically engage with everything it posts.
- On Twitter especially, think of your tweet as a headline (see chapter 6). It needs to set the theme, offer a benefit, create intrigue, ask a question or give the reader some news.
- Commands (chapter 6) in conjunction with links can work as powerful calls to action (chapter 8).
- If you're linking to something else, be very careful when using intrigue. People prefer to know where they're going before they click. Whatever is behind the link should deliver on the promise of your post.
- You write your post in isolation, but your reader will see it among hundreds of others. To give it the best chance of cutting through, keep it as simple as you can (see 'Make it simple' in chapter 12).
- Sentence fragments (see 'Make it punchy' in chapter 12) can help you reduce length without losing any information.
- Facebook posts can be longer than tweets, but that doesn't mean 'write loads'. Make the length suit the message (see 'Give information' in chapter 7 and 'Get the length right' in chapter 12).
- Offer value. What knowledge or advice could you or the client give the reader that would help them? How can you give them a good reason to share your posts?

- What do readers need to know before they can buy from you? (See 'Give information' in chapter 7.) How can you give them the information they need without being too pushy?
- Visuals get more shares, so think about ways you can include them. A related image is OK, but far better is a visual representation of what you're saying – a diagram, infographic, cartoon or something similar. (See 'Use visuals and formats' in chapter 7 and 'Use images' in chapter 9.)
- Make sure any text that appears in visuals and images is in harmony with the text of the post itself. They should feel like two halves of the same message – not a throwaway caption bolted on to a bland or pointless image.
- Be engaging. Talk to the reader in words they would use, and see things from their side. Keep your language concrete, positive and active, favouring verbs over nouns (all covered in chapter 11).
- Consider if there's a more creative way to express your message, using one or more of the ideas in chapter 9.
- Social media may be casual, but mistakes can still make a brand look bad. Check your text carefully before it's posted (see 'Check it… or get it checked' in chapter 12).
- Think very carefully before borrowing interest from current news stories or cultural events (see 'Borrow interest' in chapter 9). Are you in a position to make a useful, interesting, entertaining or insightful comment on this? If not, a 'me too' post may do more harm than good.
- Think about the other things people will be reading about in their feeds. After some major events, a respectful silence is the best and safest option. On the wrong day, a careless choice of phrase (like referring to a big mistake as a 'train wreck') could cause huge offence. Being controversial about your own brand or product is one thing; doing it

about real people's lives is something else entirely (see 'Stir it up' in chapter 9).

- If you want to use humour, choose safe subjects and make sure that what you write is actually funny (see 'Make 'em laugh' in chapter 9). Aim for a joke that only you (that is, the brand) could make (see 'Be agile' in chapter 9).
- Think about how the brand should sound on social media (see chapter 15). Social posts will probably be the most casual content written for a brand, but they should still sound like the same 'person' is speaking. Don't use things like abbreviations or emojis if they're not right for the brand. The best accounts take a brand character that's already been developed elsewhere (mainly in ads) and reinvent it for social.

18

OVER TO **YOU**

We're nearly at the end of the book. I hope you've found my advice useful. But if you've read all of it, you may have noticed that it hasn't always been that consistent.

For example, in chapter 11, I said you should use the simple, concrete language of everyday speech. But the Guinness ad I praised in chapter 9 doesn't sound like a conversation. It sounds like a poem.

In chapter 9, I said that being original would make your copy more memorable and powerful. Then, in chapter 11, I suggested that a familiar phrase might be the most effective way to reach your reader.

And in chapter 15, I showed you a selection of brands that talk in very different ways, some of which went completely against the advice I'd given you before.

So which is right?

That decision is yours. Although I've tried to make this book as simple as I can, there's no 'one size fits all' formula for copywriting.

On every new job, you have to choose the right approach for the client, the product and the project. You also have to decide what's right for you in terms of what you write, how you write it and who you write it for.

You can be a blue-sky brand writer, or a salesperson in print who's all about results. You can see your copywriting as an art form, or as a branch of behavioural science. You can lose yourself in word-love or go hunting big ideas. You can lovingly craft longform writing or hone nuggets of microcopy. You can make yourself a specialist or be a Jack (or Jill) of all trades. In the future, you may even have to decide whether to work alongside artificial intelligence or defend good old human writing against the rise of the machines.

The more of these decisions you make, the more you'll find your own way, and build up your confidence too. Over time, you'll realise what sort of copywriter you want to be, and grow into the mould you've made for yourself. Then, one day, you'll turn round, look back and realise how far you've come.

I've shown you the blank page and put the pen in your hand. What's written next is up to you.

ABOUT THE **AUTHOR**

Tom Albrighton has been a professional copywriter for over 12 years.

In that time, he's written about everything from cupcakes and cameras to spectacles and solar panels, working for household names like Prudential, Jeyes and Fuji, as well as dozens of small businesses and marketing agencies.

Tom is also a co-founder of the Professional Copywriters' Network, the UK alliance of commercial writers. In a 2015 DMA survey, he was ranked the #7 'Copywriter rated by copywriters'.